Short cut to fashion

Short cut to fashion

Short cut to fashion

Make your own clothes without buying patterns

MARTIN SHOBEN

HUTCHINSON

London   Melbourne   Sydney   Auckland   Johannesburg

Hutchinson & Co. (Publishers) Ltd

An imprint of the Hutchinson Publishing Group

17–21 Conway Street, London W1P 6JD

Hutchinson Publishing Group (Australia) Pty Ltd
16–22 Church Street, Hawthorn, Melbourne, Victoria 3122

Hutchinson Group (NZ) Ltd
32–34 View Road, PO Box 40–086, Glenfield, Auckland 10

Hutchinson Group (SA) (Pty) Ltd
PO Box 337, Bergvlei 2012, South Africa

First published 1985

© Martin M. Shoben 1985

Fashion illustrations drawn by Stephen Worth

Set in VIP Cheltenham by
D. P. Media Limited, Hitchin, Hertfordshire

Printed and bound in Great Britain by
Anchor Brendon Ltd, Tiptree, Essex

British Library Cataloguing in Publication Data
Shoben, Martin
　　Short Cut to Fashion: make your own clothes without buying patterns
　　1. Dressmaking – Pattern design
　　I. Title
　　646.4′3204　　TT520

ISBN 0 09 160881 3

Cover illustration courtesy *Family Circle*. Photograph by Richard McLaren

*For my father
Montague Shoben*

Contents

Key to symbols	8
Acknowledgements	9
Introduction	11

STYLE 1 ★★
Overshirt in cheesecloth
12

STYLE 2 ★★
Cotton overshirt
15

STYLE 3 ★
Tee shirt
17

STYLE 4 ★★
Basic kimono
20

STYLE 5 ★★★
Kaftan
24

STYLE 6 ★★★
Dress with gathered sleeve and flared skirt
28

STYLE 7 ★
Jersey blouse
32

STYLE 8 ★
Tunic dress with shoulder fastening
34

STYLE 9 ★
Tube dress draped from the shoulder
36

STYLE 10 ★
Tube dress draped from above the bust
38

STYLE 11 ★★
Kaftan 40

STYLE 12 ★★★
Day dress 42

STYLE 13 ★★
Full circle skirt 46

STYLE 14 ★★
Half circle skirt 48

STYLE 15 ★★★
A-line skirt 51

STYLE 16 ★★★
Four-panelled spiral skirt with draped hem 54

STYLE 17 ★★
Tablecloth skirt 57

STYLE 18 ★
Gathered dirndl 59

STYLE 19 ★★
Harem trousers 61

STYLE 20 ★★★
Cowl neck blouse 63

Metric measurements 67

Fibres and fabrics 68

Glossary of basic skills 72

Specialist suppliers 79

Further reading 79

Key to symbols

The stars are a guide to the difficulty of the pattern cutting and sewing of each style.

The geometric symbols show at a glance what shape the style is based on.

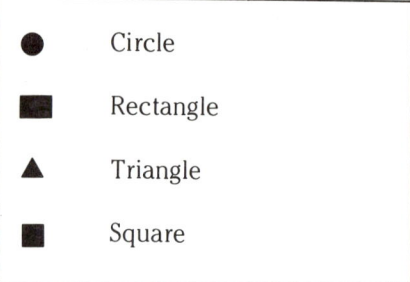

Acknowledgements

I would like to acknowledge the help received from Willi Shaer and my colleagues at the London College of Fashion in the preparation of this book, in particular Lilly Silberberg, Patrick Taylor, Janet Ward, Grace Paskin, Eunice Cain and Krystyna Ratajska for contributing some of the styles. Also my thanks to Technical Editor Anne Howes, and also Ann Evans, Paula Bayne and Doug Fox for their help and advice in the production of this book – and finally to my wife Jenny for her patience and understanding.

Introduction

This book is for dressmakers who possess a basic knowledge of garment construction and who wish to experiment with cutting their own patterns.

It contains detailed instructions for cutting and making a versatile, original wardrobe of clothes that are to a large extent classical and have a timeless quality. The theme linking the styles together is that they are all cut from basic shapes, the rectangle, the triangle, the circle or the square, and that they are all loosely fitting and comfortable to wear. All that is required to cut and sew these clothes is a rudimentary knowledge of dressmaking, such as sewing a straight line, inserting a zip and the ability to measure and accurately draw straight lines. All these skills are illustrated in the Glossary which can be found towards the back of the book.

Each style is more or less self-contained. Hints are given as to the best, most suitable fabrics to choose, how to fold and cut the fabric and the sequence of sewing for each garment. Styles are graded according to difficulty by the use of a star system. One star is the easiest and three stars the hardest. However, all the styles are readily achievable and should prove an interesting pastime and an enjoyable, profitable experience.

Some of the styles (usually the easiest) can be cut simply by folding the fabric (but note that nap and one-way fabrics present problems when folded. So choose your fabrics with care), while other styles need a paper pattern. Paper patterns can, of course, be used again and again, so that, after working through the styles, an interesting set of patterns can be built up and stored. By varying the fabrics, many beautiful styles can be produced.

Style 1
Overshirt in cheesecloth

STYLE 1

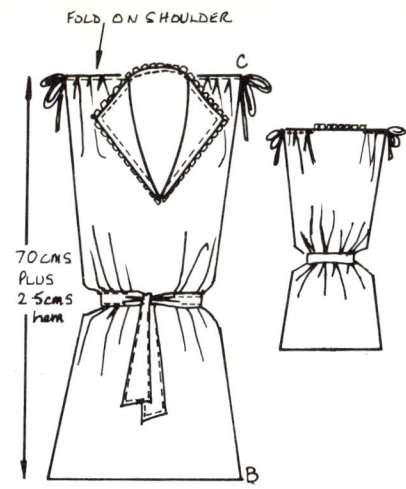

Figure 1

This overshirt is an attractive, simple garment that will look good with many types of separates, such as shorts, skirts, jeans or culottes. It is very easy to cut and is developed from a pure rectangle, the dimensions of which are based on fabric width and fashion length.

FABRIC

Cheesecloth or similar cotton fabric, but the width must be at least 112 cm to obtain the gathering required around the bust/chest.

FABRIC LENGTH

Decide garment length, i.e. from shoulder to hem; the fabric length required is twice this length plus allowances for the hem, normally 5 cm. Therefore, if the garment length is 70 cm from shoulder to hem, the meterage will be 70 × 2 = 140 cm plus 5 cm for the hem = 140 + 5 = 145 cm.

PATTERN

A pattern will not be needed for this garment, just mark directly on to the fabric. Measurements given include seam allowances.

TRIMMINGS

Braid or ribbon to finish off the armholes and neckline if required.

CUTTING OUT

See Figures 3, 4, 5 and 6.

MAKING UP

See Figures 7 and 8.

MEASUREMENTS REQUIRED

Figure 2

1. Measure around the wearer's bust/chest and allow 20 cm for looseness around the body. This 20 cm will allow the garment to be suitable for sizes 10 –18, but obviously the larger sizes will have fewer gathers, to be drawn in at the shoulders.

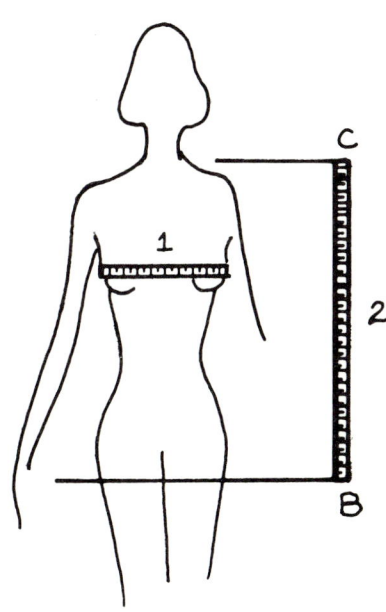

Figure 2

2. Measure from the shoulder to the required fashion length, add hem allowances, double the measurement to calculate the fabric length required (see fabric length). Carefully lay the fabric on to the table.

Figure 3

The open fabric:
Mark line A–B with chalk or pins and then cut along A–B. Retain the cut strip for ties and crossway at neck and armholes and tie belt, if not using braid or other trimmings.

Figure 4

1. Line C–C is where the overshirt will eventually fold down to form the shirt length, i.e. C–B.
2. With chalk or pins mark a lengthwise centre line on which point D is located.

Figure 5

Point D is located halfway along C–C.

Figure 6

1. *Neck opening.* Mark the following points with chalk:
The neckline D–E = 9 cm – both ways
  D–F = 2 cm
  D–G = 19 cm
Cut along G–D–E–F–E–D for neckline.
2. Armhole depth. Mark point H which is 30 cm down from C on shoulder.

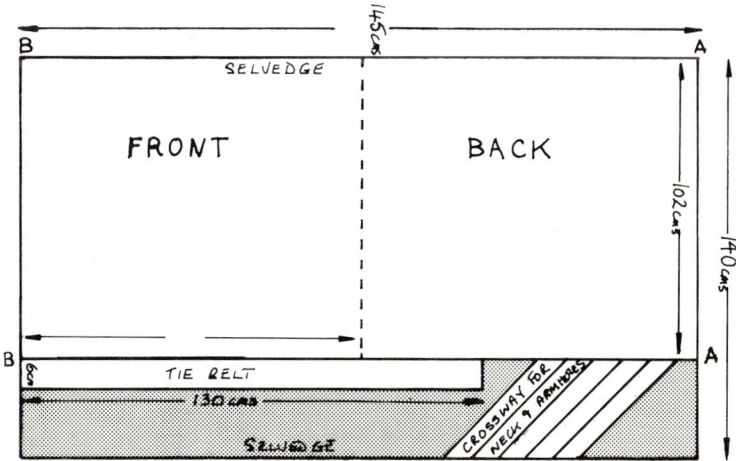

Figure 3

STYLE 1

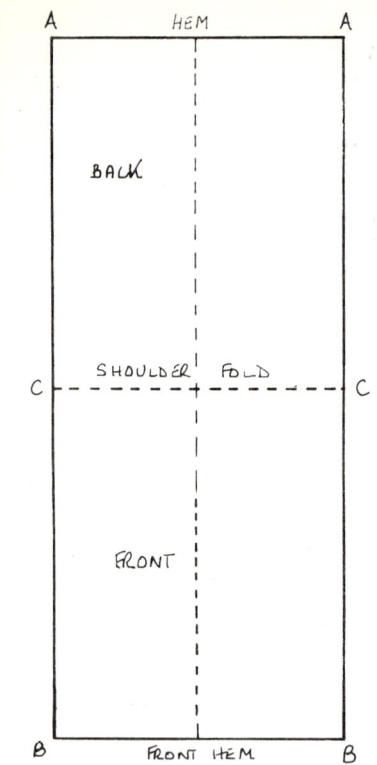

Figure 4

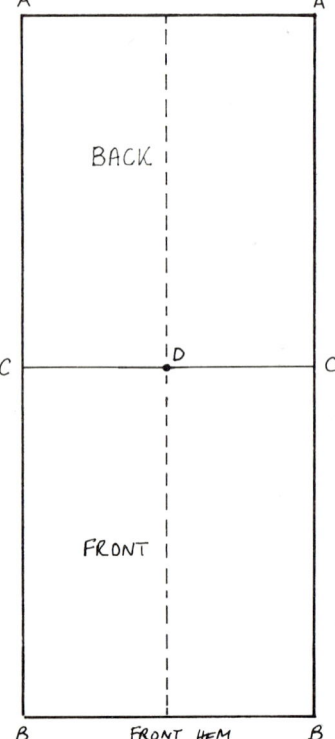

Figure 5

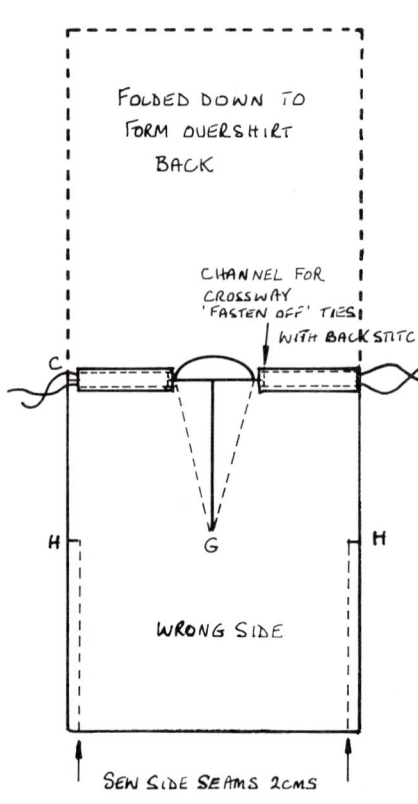

Figure 6

Figure 7

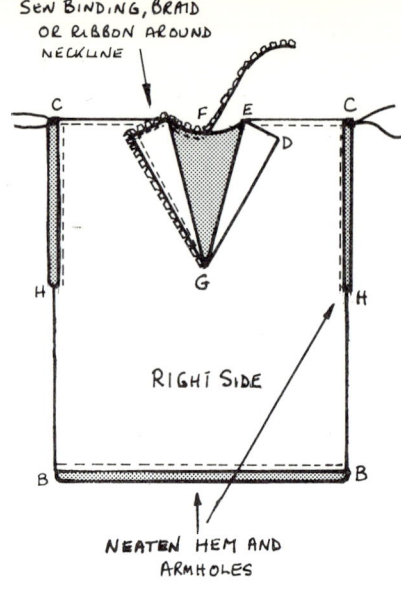

Figure 8

Figure 7

Channels for the ties at shoulder:
1. Cut a channel for the ties, the length of the shoulder by 5 cm.
2. Bag out and turn through.
3. Sew channel to inside of garment shoulder and insert ties and fasten at neckline point E.

The side seam:
Fold down the back and sew side seams up to the armhole mark.

Figure 8

Press open side seams and turn garment through to right side. Turn back neckline and neaten edge or sew on braid, crossway, or ribbons as desired.

Note If binding is used measure G–D–E–F–E–D–G × 3 cm wide and apply to neckline, but remember to stitch it on to the neckline (see page 73, Glossary of basic skills). Neaten hem and armholes with binding if required or simply neaten seam edges and turn up once. Cut tie belt required length by 6 cm, stitch and turn through (see Glossary of basic skills). To arrange the gathers place the overshirt on to the wearer and gather the shoulder up, fasten by tying a knot in the ties and fastening securely.

STYLE 2

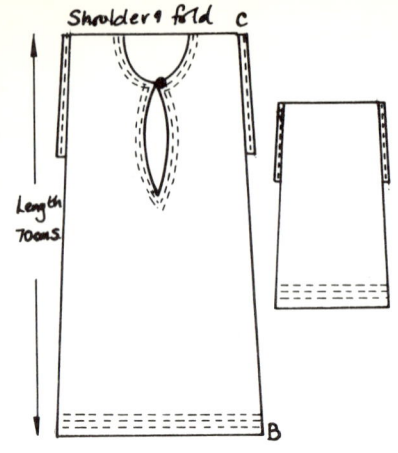

Figure 9

This overshirt is very similar to Style 1. It is developed from a rectangle the size of which will depend on the size of the wearer.

FABRIC

Cotton, cheesecloth etc. The width is determined by how loose the shirt is required to fit. 90 cm wide fabric will be suitable for an average adult woman size 12.

FABRIC LENGTH

Decide garment length from shoulder to hem. Double this and add hem allowance, for example, garment length 70 cm × 2 = 140 cm plus 10 cm = 150 cm.

PATTERN

A pattern is not required, just mark directly on to the fabric. Measurements given include seam allowances.

TRIMMINGS

One button to fasten neckline.

CUTTING OUT

See Figures 11, 12 and 13.

MAKING UP

See Figure 14 and Glossary of basic skills.

MEASUREMENTS REQUIRED

Figure 10

1. Measure around the bust/chest and allow 20 cm for looseness around the body. Divide this in half to calculate the width of the overshirt, e.g. bust 86 cm – half of this is 43 cm, plus a minimum of 20 cm = 63 cm.
2. Decide on a comfortable, fashionable length and remember to add an allowance for the hem.

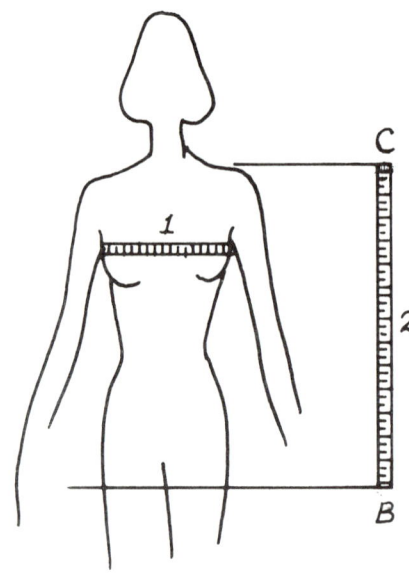

Figure 10

Figure 11

The open fabric:
With chalk, mark line A–C–B and then cut the spare strip away. Retain the spare strip of fabric for armhole and neck finishing.

Figure 12

Draw line D–E halfway between A–A.
Draw line C–C halfway between A–B.

The neckline:
Establish point F (the exact centre of rectangle).
G–F = 2 cm
H–F = 8 cm
I–F = 7.5 cm (both ways)
J–H = 10 cm

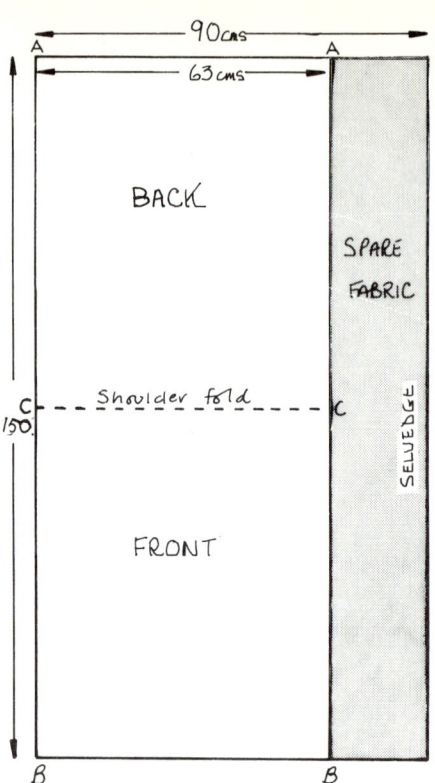

Figure 11

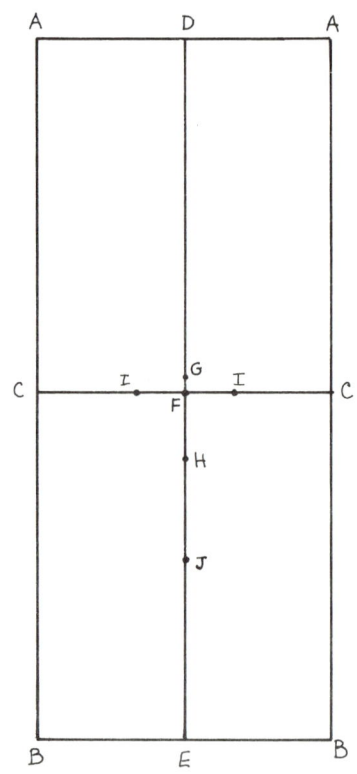

Figure 12

Figure 13

Draw back and front neckline by connecting points G–I–H–J as shown, use a French curve if necessary.
Cut away neckline.
Mark points K and L for armhole

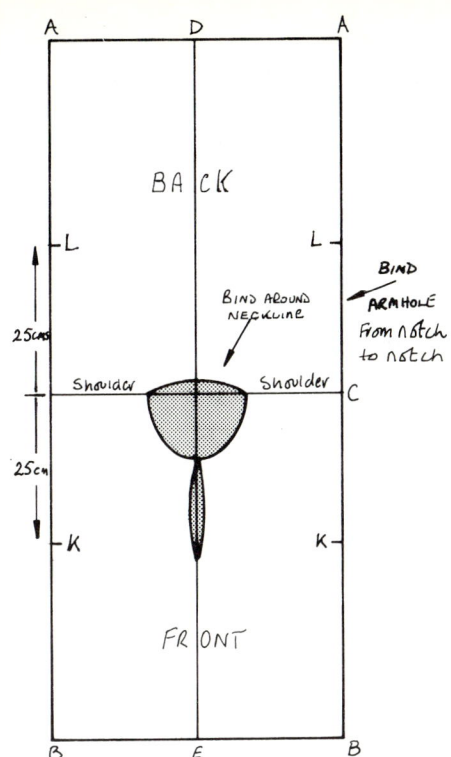

Figure 13

depth 25 cm down from shoulder line.
Cut spare fabric into strips on the cross, see page 73 and sew around neckline and along armholes.

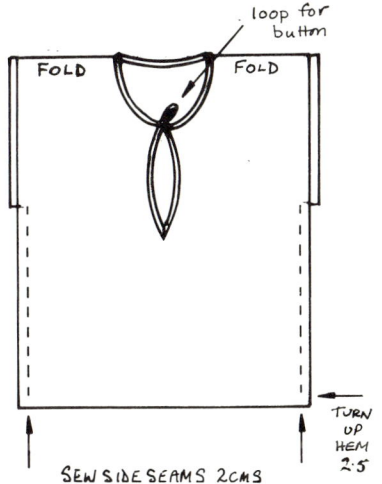

Figure 14

Figure 14
After binding armholes and neckline, fold garment in half at shoulder and sew side seams and then finally turn up the hem and stitch if required.
Sew button at neck.

Note The style is shown with rows of topstitching. This is optional.

Style 3
Tee shirt

STYLE 3

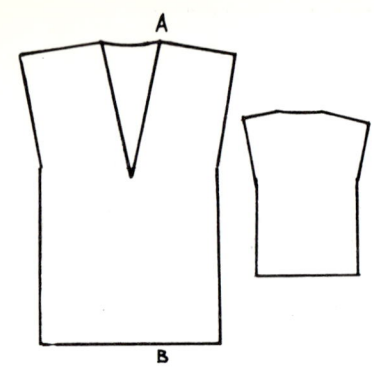

Figure 15

This tee shirt is always fashionable and is extremely simple to construct and sew.

FABRIC

Any soft fabric will be suitable.

FABRIC LENGTH

60 cm of any width fabric for a size 12.

PATTERN

A pattern is required for this garment. You will need a large sheet of pattern paper.

TRIMMINGS

None.

CUTTING OUT

See Figure 21.

MAKING UP

See Figure 22 and Glossary of basic skills.

MEASUREMENTS REQUIRED

Figure 16

1. Measure around the bust/chest and allow 20 cm for looseness around the body. Divide this in half to calculate the width of the pattern, e.g. bust 86 cm plus 20 cm tolerance = 106 cm, divide this in half = 53 cm.

2. The garment length, i.e. from shoulder to hem (this is a matter of choice, but decide on a comfortable, fashionable length), in this example 55 cm.

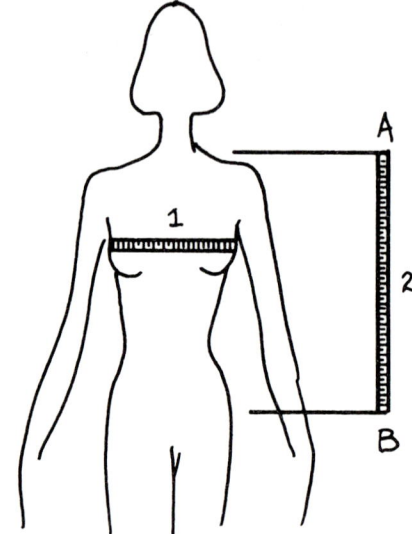

Figure 16

Figure 17

Construct the basic rectangle on paper:
1. On a large sheet of paper construct a rectangle 53 cm wide × 55 cm long.
2. Draw line A–B which will be the centre line.
3. Mark point C which is 9 cm from A.
4. Mark point D which is 21 cm (this can be varied according to the required neckline depth).
5. Mark point E, 2 cm down from A for back neck.

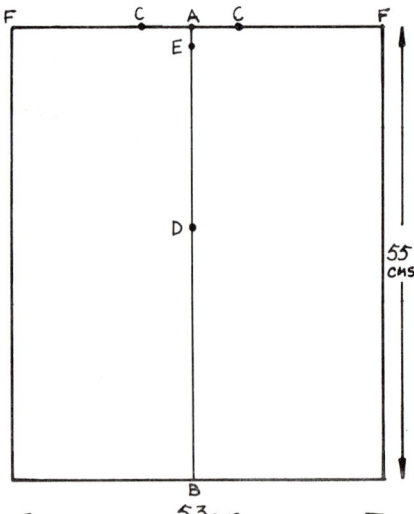

Figure 17

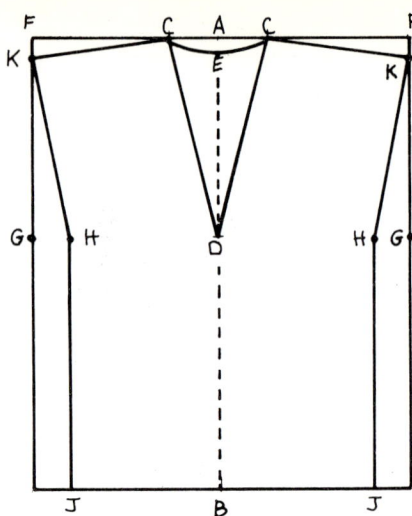

Figure 18

Figure 18

Plan the style:
Connect C–E for back neckline.
Mark point G for armhole depth 21 cm down from F.
H from G = 2.5 cm.
Drop a line down to J at hem.
K is 2 cm from F – for shoulder slope.

Figure 19

Trace off the front pattern and add seam allowances:
On to another sheet of paper trace-off points B–D–C–K–H–J for half of the front tee shirt.
Add seam allowances all around the outline and cut out the pattern.

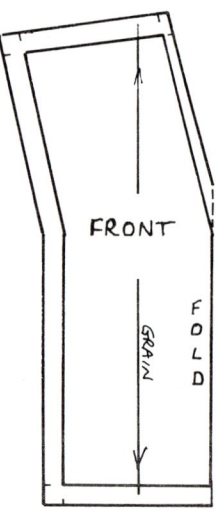

Figure 19

18

STYLE 3

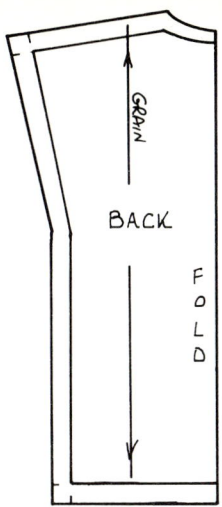

Figure 20

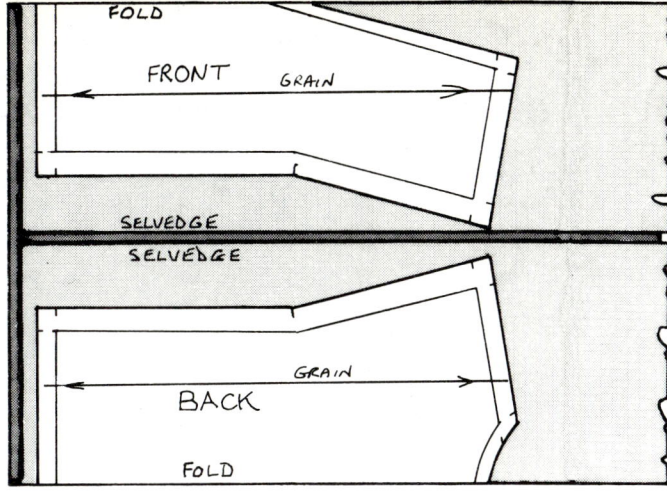

Figure 21

Figure 20

Trace off the back pattern and add seam allowances:
On to another sheet of paper trace-off points
B–D–E–C–K–H–J for half of the back tee shirt.
Add seam allowances all around the outline and cut out the pattern.

FABRIC LAYOUT

Figure 21

1. Lay fabric flat on to the table.
2. Fold selvedges inwards towards centre.
3. Lay the front and back patterns on to the fabric as shown in Figure 21.
4. Mark around the pattern or, alternatively, pin the pattern down to the fabric.
5. Using sharp shears cut very carefully around the pattern.

ASSEMBLY SEQUENCE

Figure 22

1. Overlock or neaten all around the front and back tee shirt.
2. Sew side seams.
3. Sew shoulder seams.
4. Neaten neckline and armholes by turning up a tiny hem and sewing.
5. Turn up the required hem and sew.
6. Press.

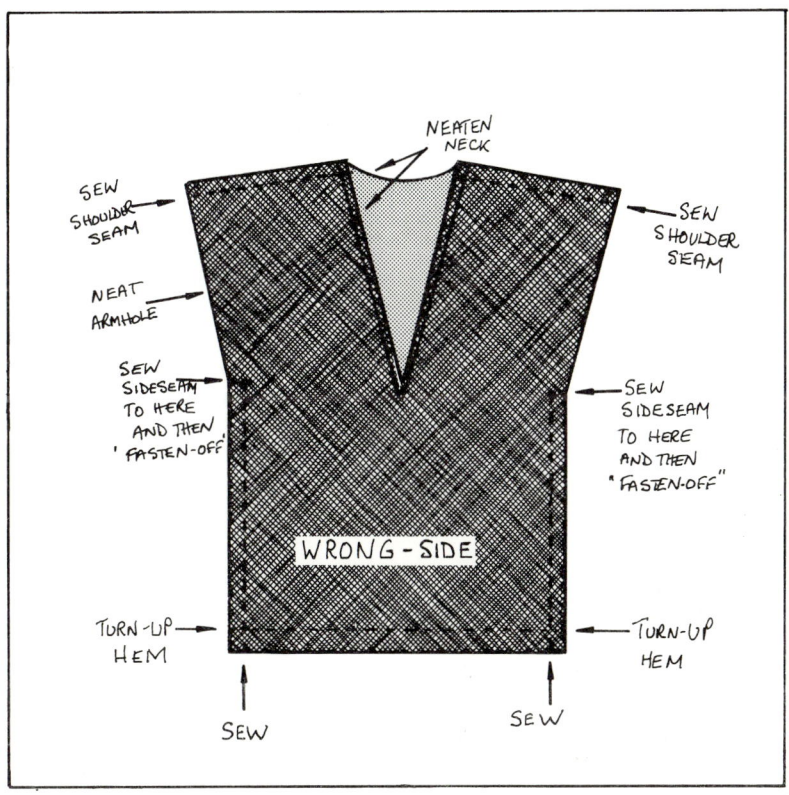

Figure 22

STYLE 4

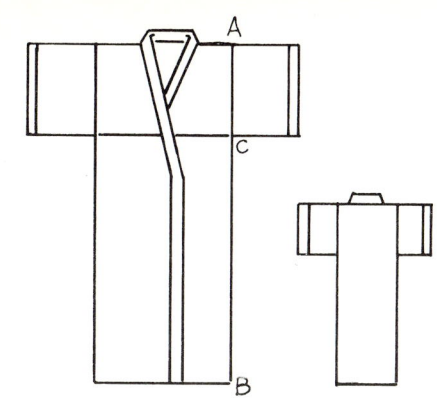

Figure 23

This style forms the basis of some of the styles contained in this book. It is very similar to the traditional Japanese kimono and is an extremely wearable attractive garment. Ideal as a bathrobe, overshirt etc., it also has the advantage of being multi-sized and unisex.

FABRIC

Almost any fabric is suitable for this style as long as the minimum width is 122 cm. Wrap the fabric around the intended wearer to check that it will be full and loose enough. Use any contrast fabric for belt and neck finish.

FABRIC LENGTH

The length of the finished garment plus the sleeve depth and the hem allowance (see Figures 24 and 25) and belt if in the same fabric.

FABRIC WIDTH

Minimum width for an adult would be 122 cm. However, if a 90 cm fabric is used it would be possible to cut the kimono along the selvedge so that the garment would be shorter, for example, 90 cm minus sleeve depth – perhaps ideal for a child.

PATTERN

A pattern is not needed for this style, simply fold the fabric as shown. Seam allowances are included in the fabric dimension. Practise folding paper before using your fabric.

CUTTING OUT

See Figures 25 to 30.

MAKING UP

See Figure 34 and Glossary of basic skills.

MEASUREMENTS REQUIRED

Figure 24

1. A to B: measure from the shoulder to the hem length required, add hem allowances.
2. A–C is the sleeve depth.
3. Measure around the hip (the fullest part of the body) and make sure that the width of the fabric from selvedge to selvedge is loose enough. The overall length is therefore A + B + C.

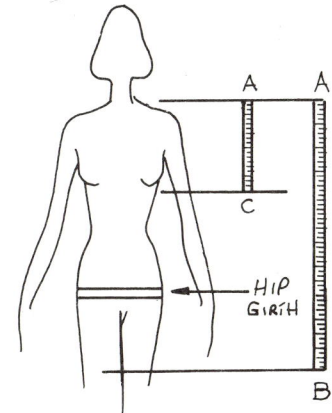

Figure 24

Examples:
1 A–B is   77 cm
2 A–C is   30 cm
            _____
            107 cm
   plus hem 3 cm
            _____
            110 cm
   plus belt 10 cm
            _____
            120 cm is the overall
                   length plus width
                   of fabric.

Also cut crossway to finish neck, either self or contrast.

Figure 25

Cut a length of fabric to the dimensions calculated in Figure 24.

Figure 26

Fold the sleeve width downwards and carefully crease and pin to hold firmly.

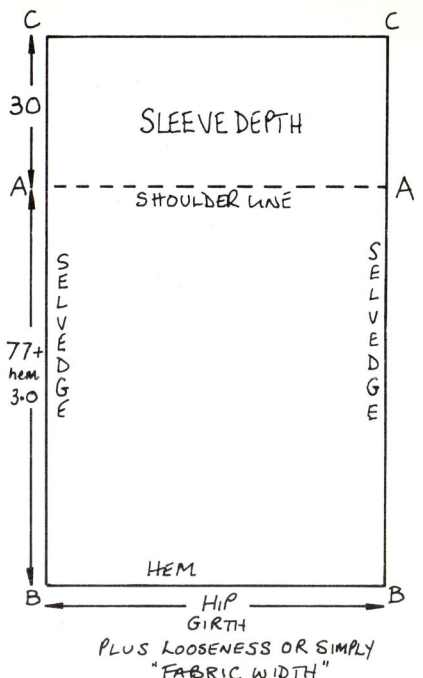

Figure 25

Figure 27

Fold the fabric in half lengthwise, i.e. selvedge way, and then cut out the back neck, through all the fabric thicknesses.

Figure 28

Open out the fabric.

Figure 29

Cut from point D at the back neck to E on the centre front, fold for the front neck.

Figure 30

Open out the fabric.

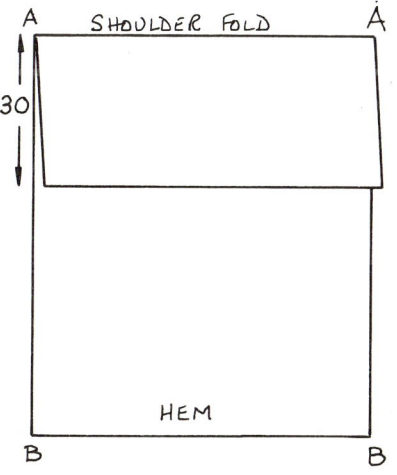

Figure 26

STYLE 4

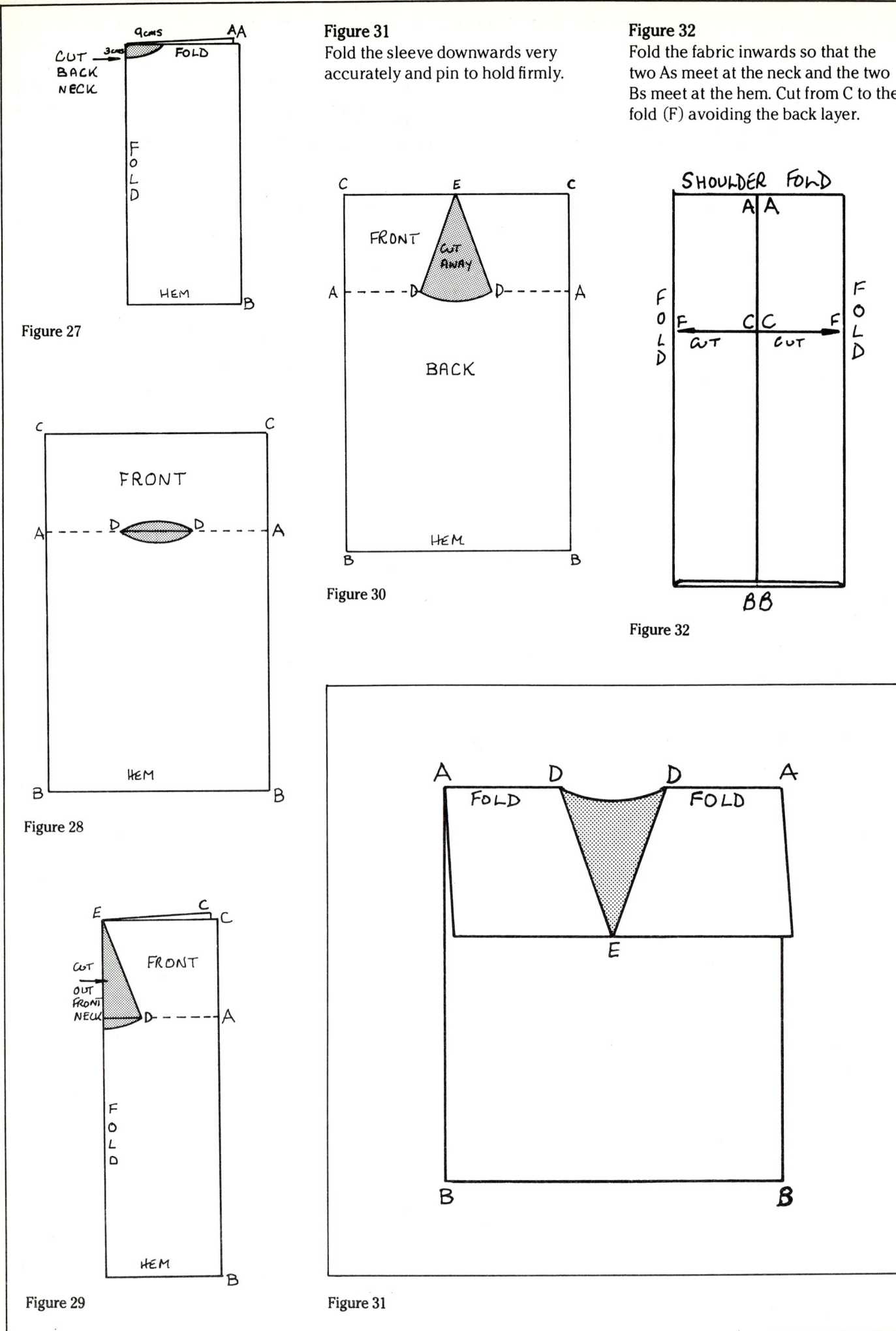

Figure 31
Fold the sleeve downwards very accurately and pin to hold firmly.

Figure 32
Fold the fabric inwards so that the two As meet at the neck and the two Bs meet at the hem. Cut from C to the fold (F) avoiding the back layer.

Figure 27

Figure 28

Figure 29

Figure 30

Figure 32

Figure 31

STYLE 4

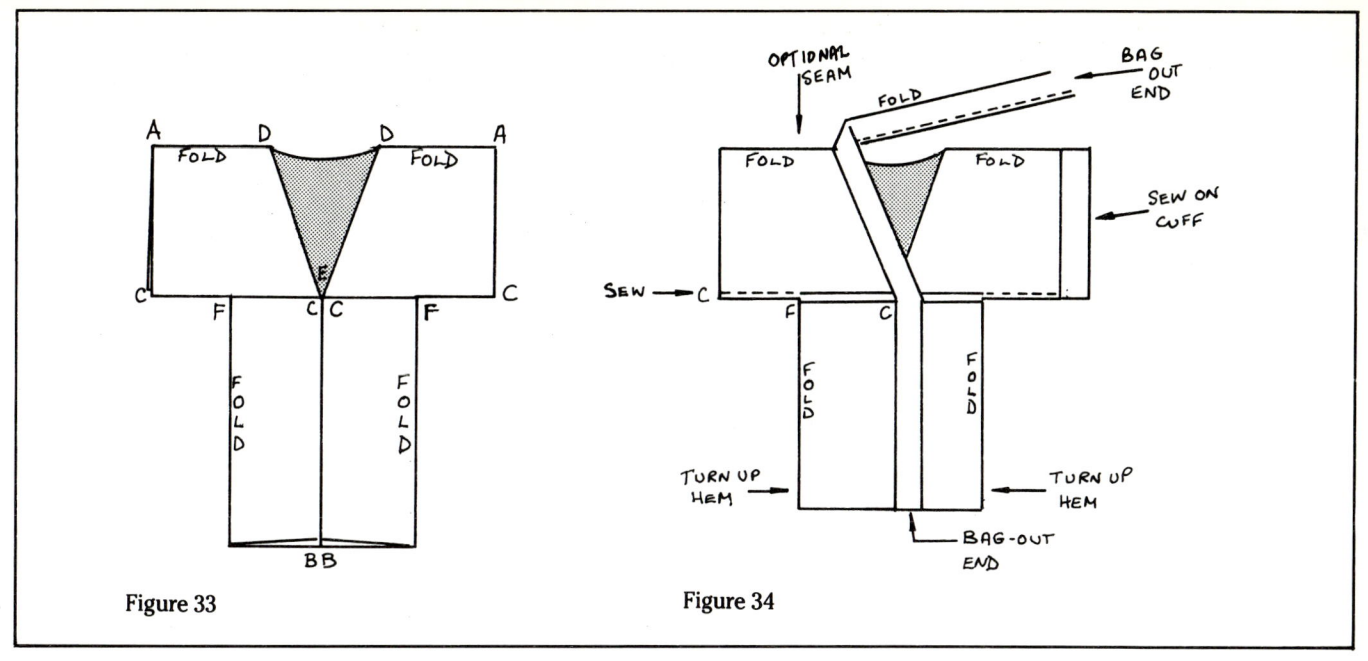

Figure 33

Figure 34

Figure 33
Open out C to F to obtain sleeve.

ASSEMBLY SEQUENCE

Figure 34
1. Sew sleeve underarm from C to F both sides.
2. Join F to C by either top stitching a braid to cover seam or 'pinch out' a small seam either side of the cut.
3. Finish the centre front and neckline by joining a long crossway strip of approximately 5 cm finished width, therefore cut a strip 11 cm wide × 172 cm long in either self fabric or contrast.
4. Finish sleeve end by joining a straight strip of fabric to the sleeve ends 60 cm × 11 cm two pieces.
5. A tie belt could be made in the length required and the same width as the neck and cuffs.
6. Turn up hem.

STYLE 5

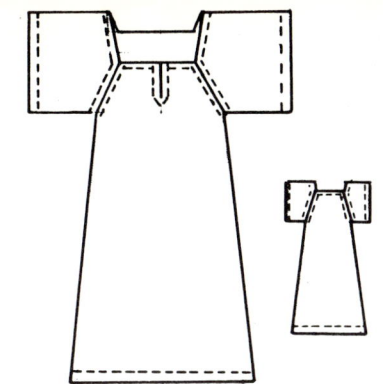

Figure 35

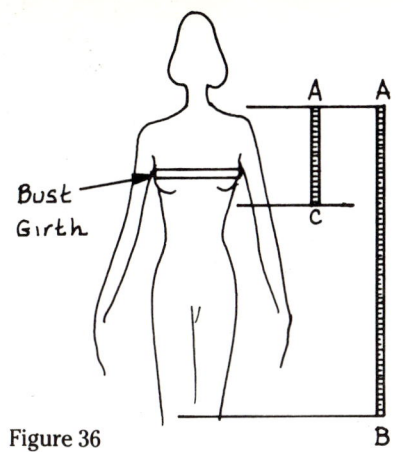

Figure 36

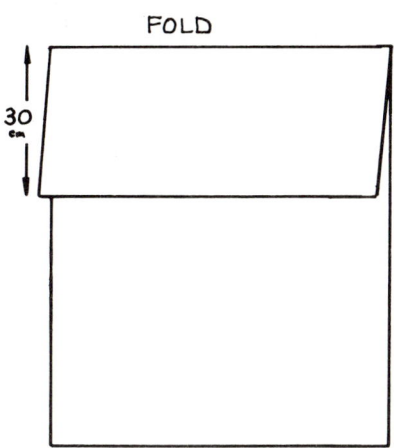

Figure 38
Fold down sleeve depth.

Figure 38

This kaftan is developed the same way as the previous style. The only difference is that the centre front and the centre back seams are taken away and side seams and shoulder seams are added. Vary the length and width according to choice and size of wearer.

FABRIC

Any soft fabric will be suitable.

FABRIC LENGTH

This will depend on the garment length, fabric width and sleeve depth. The meterage for a size 12 is approximately 150 cm on a wide fabric, e.g. 150 cm width.

PATTERN

A pattern is required for this dress.

TRIMMINGS

None.

CUTTING OUT

See layout in Figure 48.

MAKING UP

See sequence of assembly, Figure 49 and Glossary of basic skills.

MEASUREMENTS REQUIRED

Figure 36
1. A–B: measure from the shoulder to the hem length required, add hem allowances.
2. A–C is the sleeve depth. Measure around the bust, and add at least 20 cm.
The example illustrated here will measure as follows:
Length   A–B = 100 cm
Sleeve depth   A–C = 30 cm
Bust   86 + 20 cm = 106 cm

Figure 37
Cut a length of paper 130 cm long by 106 cm wide.

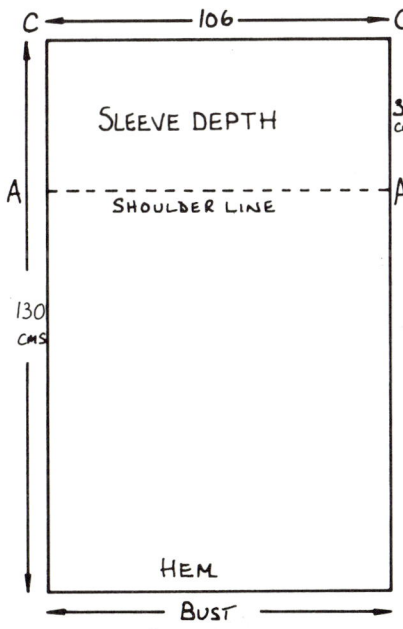

Figure 37

Figure 39
Fold the paper in half lengthways and cut out back neck 6 cm down and 12 cm in.

Figure 40
Open out the paper and carefully mark the centre line.

Figure 41
Again fold the paper in half lengthwise and cut out front neck, i.e. an extra 6 cm.

Figure 42
Open out the paper and fold down the sleeve depth.

Figure 43
Fold both edges inwards so that the As and the two Bs and two Cs meet on centre line. Cut from C to D (on the long fold) avoiding the back layer of paper.

Figure 44
Open out basic kaftan.

Figure 45
To alter the seams:
1. Lay out a large sheet of paper.
2. Divide the pattern lengthways in half, i.e. down the centre front, and cut and retain the right half.
3. Pin the half pattern on to the paper.
4. Extend side seam by E–F = 8 cm. Connect F to D and D to G for sleeve style seam.

STYLE 5

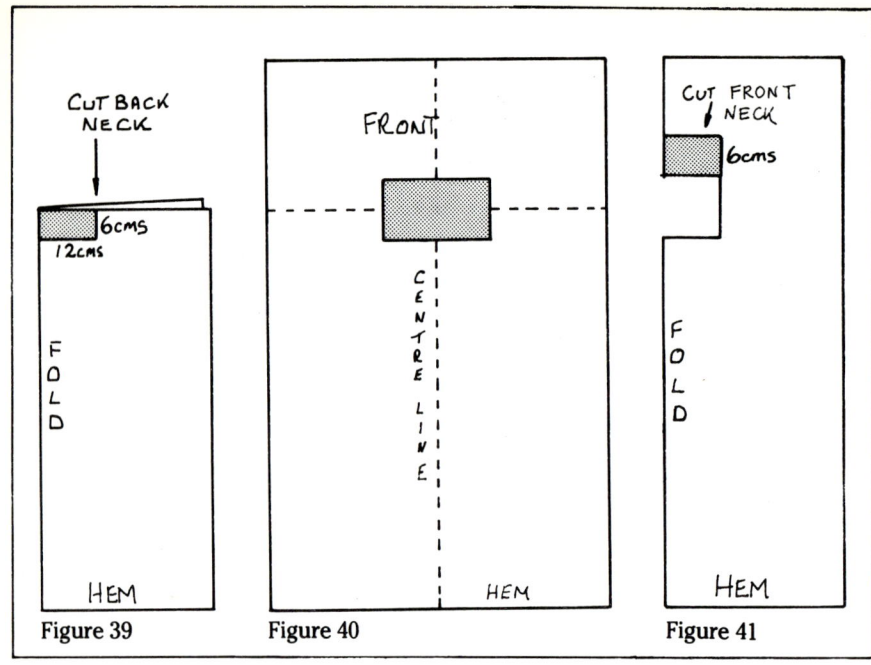

Figure 39   Figure 40   Figure 41

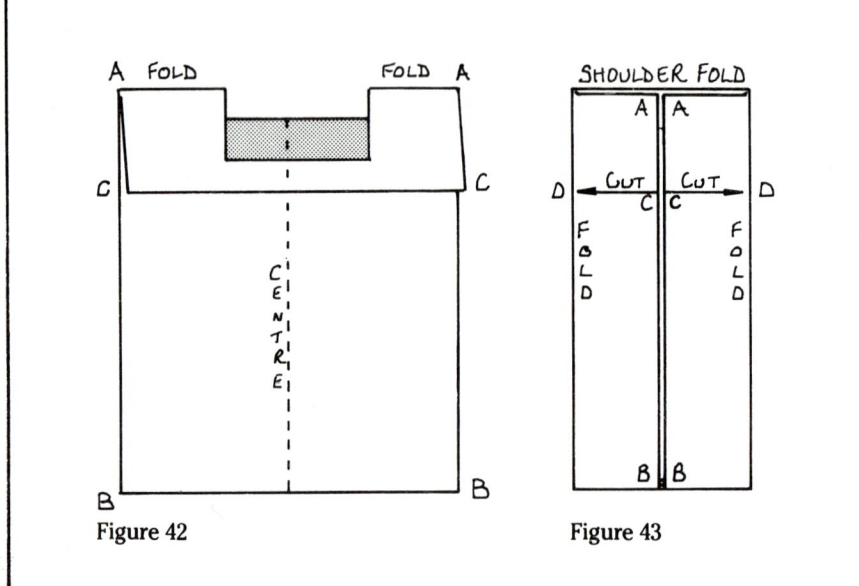

Figure 42   Figure 43

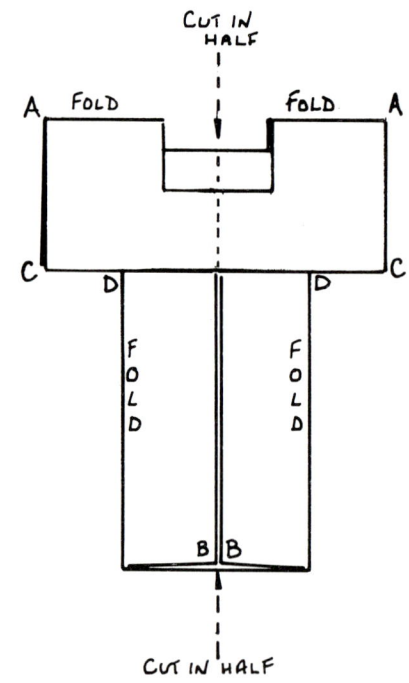

Figure 44

FABRIC LAYOUT

Figure 48
Fold the fabric inwards so that the selvedges meet. Pin the pattern as shown in Figure 48 and cut out accurately.

ASSEMBLY SEQUENCE

Figure 49
1. With garment completely open and flat, sew front and back seams of sleeves to front and back kaftan.
2. Fold at sleeves so that the garment looks the same as Figure 49 with right sides inside.
3. Sew side seams and underarm seams.
4. Face neck, back and front and slit at front for the opening. See page 76 in Glossary of basic skills.
5. Turn up sleeve hems and kaftan hem.
6. Press.
7. If decorative stitching is required, stitch at this stage.

5. Mark through all these points on to the underpaper, i.e. G–H–J–F–D–G and then connect up for the front kaftan pattern.
6. Remove the original pattern.

Figure 46
1. Turn the original pattern over and lay down on to another sheet of paper. Pin firmly down.
2. Extend side seam by K–L = 8 cm.
3. Connect K to D for side seam. Connect D to M for sleeve seam.

4. Mark through points K–D–M–N–P–K to the underpaper and then connect them up for the back kaftan pattern.
5. Remove original pattern and retain for future styles.

Figure 47
Separate all sections by cutting out front and back kaftans and opening out the sleeve.
Add seam allowances as indicated in Figure 47.

STYLE 5

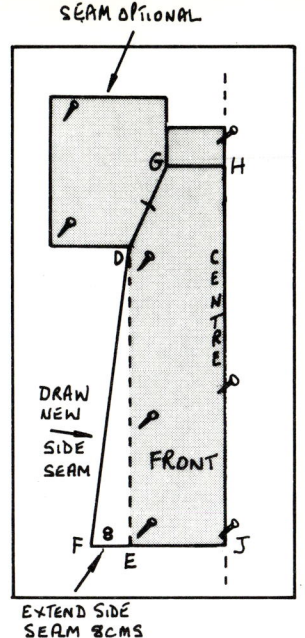

Figure 45

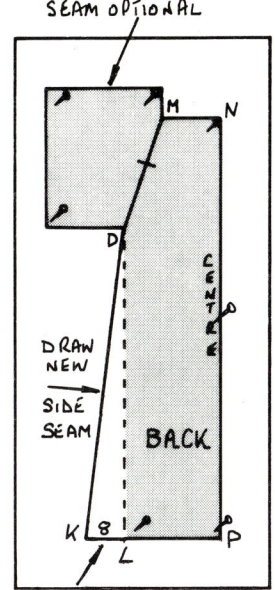

Figure 46

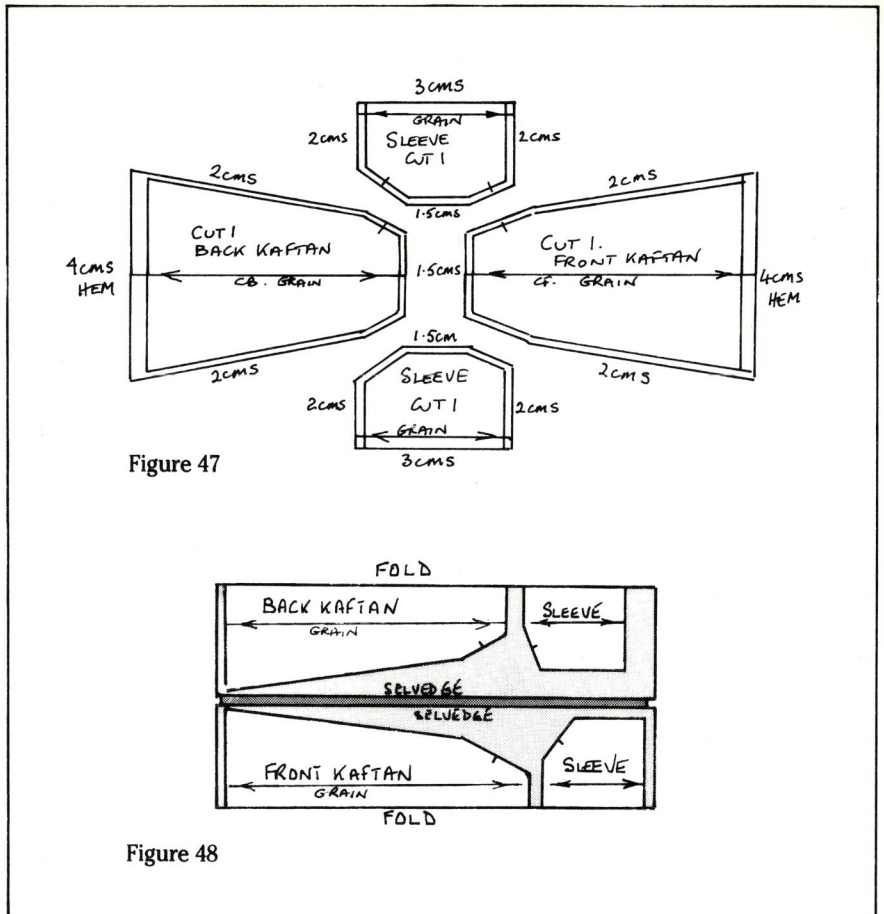

Figure 47

Figure 48

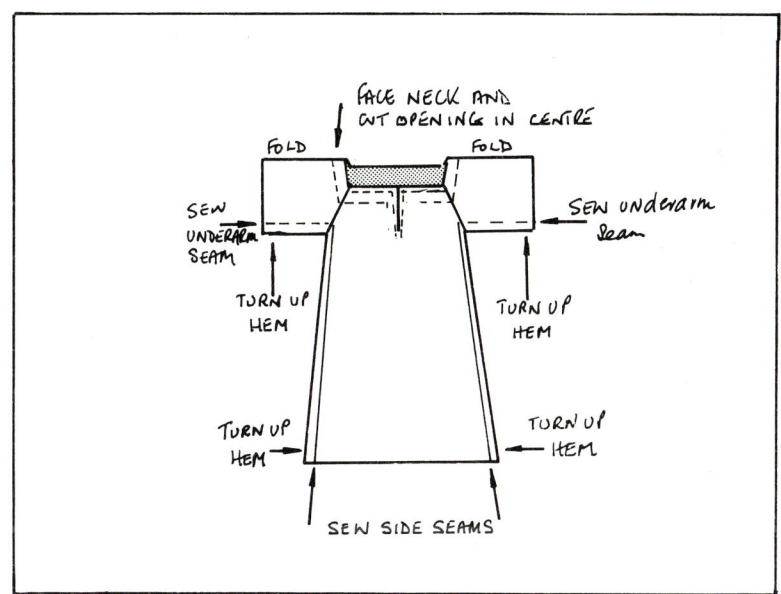

Figure 49

27

STYLE 6

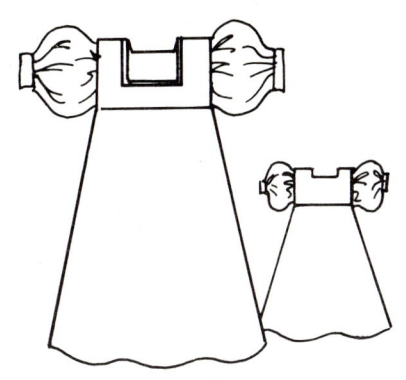

Figure 50

Another variation of the kimono, which has been developed by adding fullness into the sleeve and flaring the skirt. Follow the same sequence as Styles 4 and 5.

FABRIC

A soft fabric is desirable for this style because of the gathered sleeve and gently flared skirt.

FABRIC LENGTH

Approximately 3 metres for a size 12 using 90 cm fabric.

PATTERN

A pattern will be needed for this garment.

TRIMMINGS

None.

CUTTING OUT

See layout in Figure 64.

MAKING UP

See assembly sequence and Glossary of basic skills.

MEASUREMENTS REQUIRED

Figure 51

1. A–B. Measure from the shoulder to the required hem length.
2. A–C is the position where the across front and back seams are positioned and also the sleeve depth.
3. Measure around the bust and add at least 20 cm for tolerance. The example illustrated here will measure as follows:
   (a) Length A–B 100 cm.
   (b) Seam across bust A–C = 24 cm (also sleeve depth).
      Bust 86 cm + 20 cm = 106 cm.
4. Measure around the fullest part of the bicep to establish cuff measurement plus 2 cm ease.

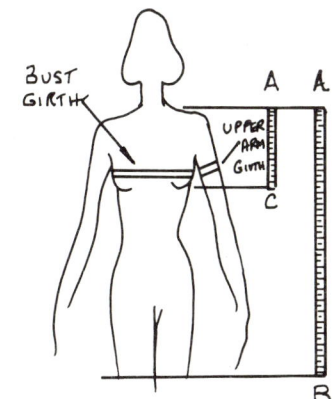

Figure 51

Figure 52

Cut a length of paper 124 cm × 106 cm.

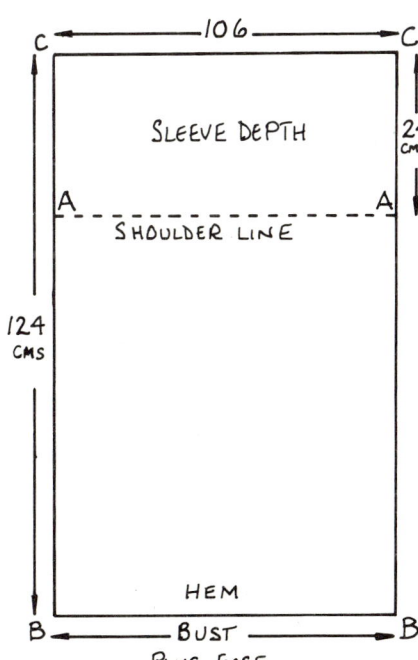

Figure 52

Figure 53

Fold down sleeve depth and crease accurately.

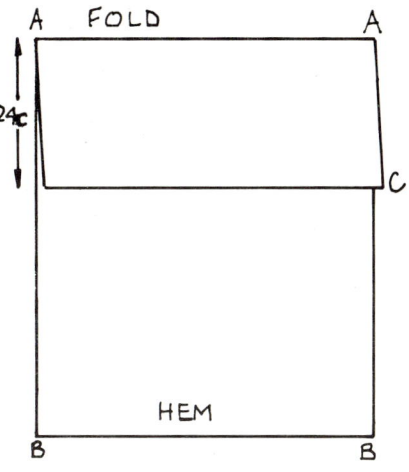

Figure 53

Figure 54

Fold the paper in half and cut out back neck as shown in Figure 54.

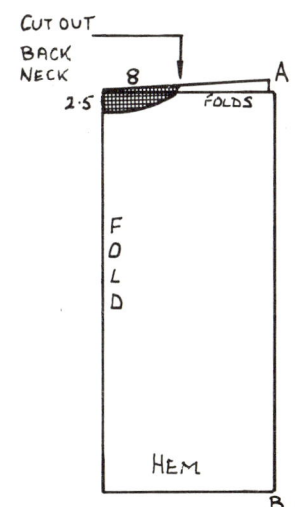

Figure 54

Figure 55

Open out the paper and carefully mark the centre line.

Figure 56

Again fold paper in half lengthways and cut out front neck an extra 12 cm.

Figure 57

Open out the paper and fold down the sleeve depth. The dotted line D is the position of the side seam, E is at the junction of lines C–D.

29

STYLE 6

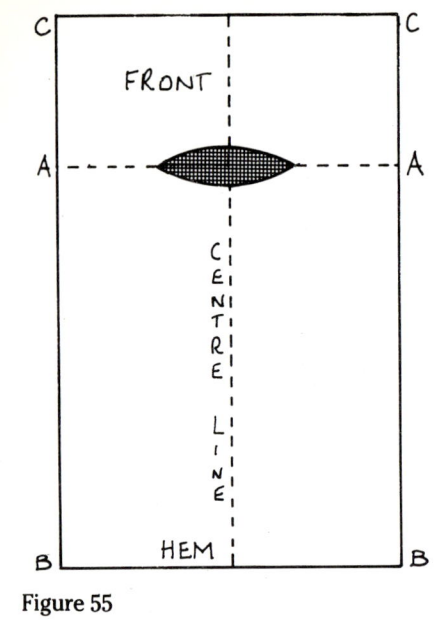

Figure 55

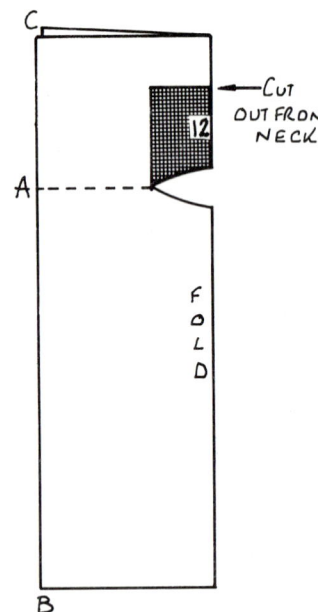

Figure 56

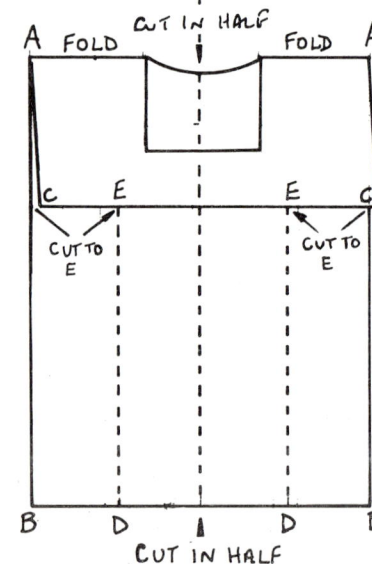

Figure 57

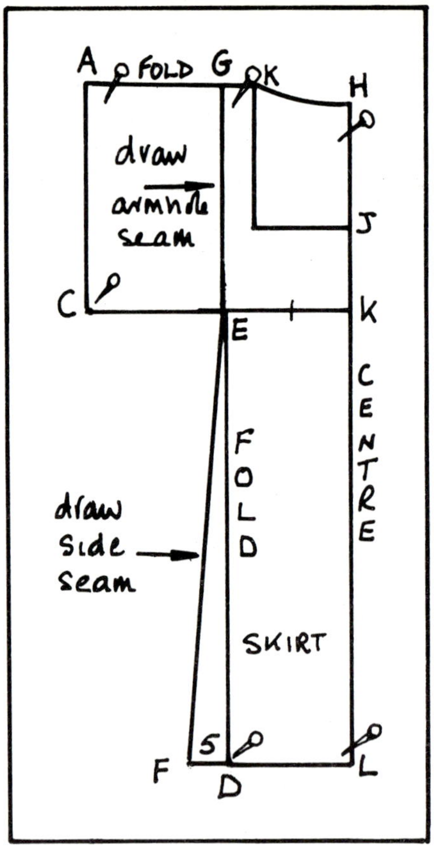

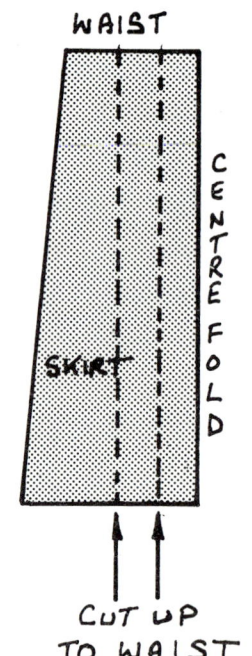

Figure 58
Pin on to another large sheet of paper. Cut along C–E and fold inwards to centre line. Only half a pattern is needed so cut away the left half of the pattern.

Figure 59

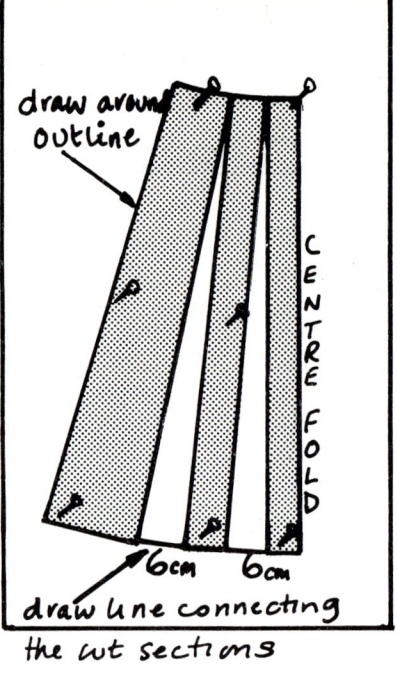

Figure 59

Altering the seams and increasing the sleeve and skirt:
F from D = 5 cm for added flare to side seam.
Connect F to E for side seam.
Connect E to G for armhole seam.
Letter all the points as shown in Figure 59 to make the next stage easier.

Trace-off the pattern and increase the sleeve and skirt as follows:
Lay a large sheet of paper flat on to the table.

Figure 60

Front skirt:
To flare the front skirt follow this sequence.
1. On to another sheet of paper trace-off the skirt section E–K–L–F–E.
2. Lay this on to the sheet of paper.
3. Divide the skirt pattern into three equal sections.
4. Slash up the pattern from hem to waist line and open out the sections so that they increase the hem by approximately 6 cm into each slash. Pin on to the sheet of paper and draw around the outline.
5. This pattern can now be used for the back and front skirt. Add seam allowances all round.

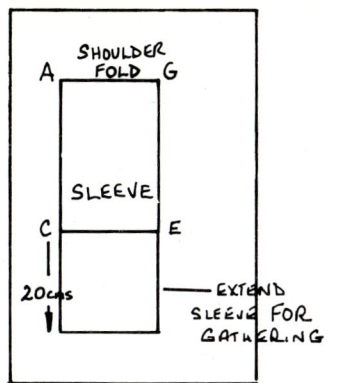

Figure 61

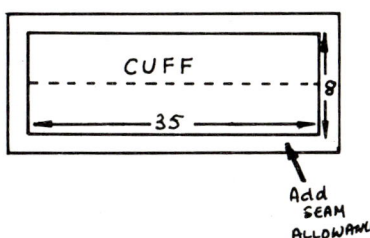

Figure 62

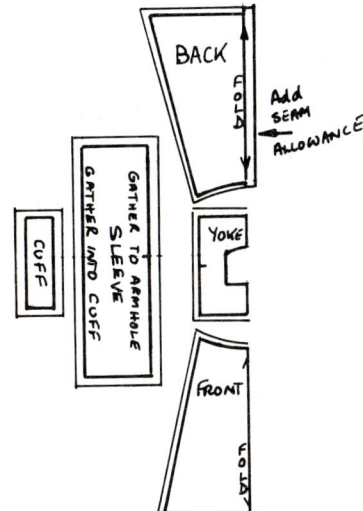

Figure 63

Figure 61

The sleeve:
1. Trace-off the sleeve from the original draft letters G–A–C–E–G.
2. Extend lines A–C and G–E by 20 cm to allow for gathering back into the armhole.
Add seam allowances to all pattern sections.

Figure 62

The cuff:
Cut the cuff according to the upper arm measurement plus ease.

Figure 63
This shows the entire pattern, indicating seam allowances.

Figure 64
This shows the suggested layout.

ASSEMBLY SEQUENCE

1. Sew binding around the neck.
2. Join the seam in the back skirt and press open.
3. Gather sleeve to armhole measurement and sew to the flat yoke (see Glossary of basic skills).
4. Join front and back skirt to the yokes.
5. Fold garment inside out and sew the side seams and underarm seams.
6. Gather sleeve to cuff (see Glossary of basic skills).
7. Press seams open.
8. Neaten seams as required (see page 76).

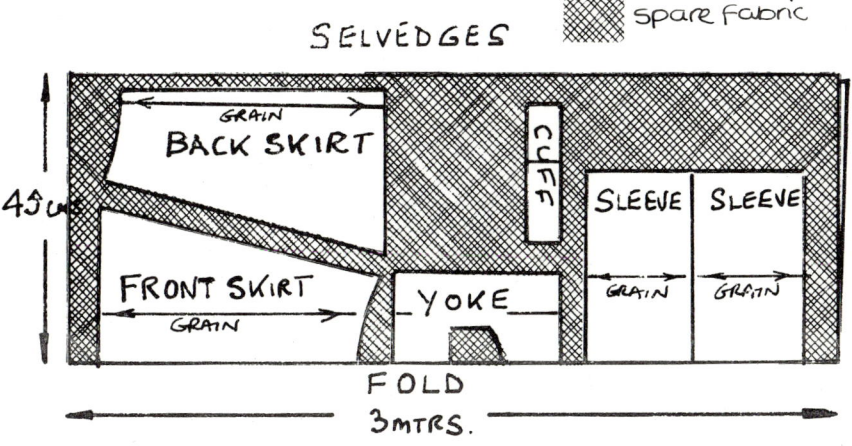

Figure 64

Style 7
Jersey blouse

STYLE 7

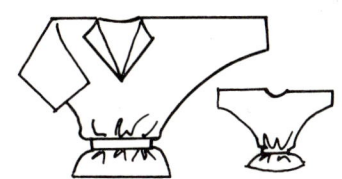

Figure 65

This very loose comfortable jersey blouse does not require a paper pattern. It is simply made by folding fabric and applying some basic measurements. The result is a very attractive blouse for mother or daughter.

FABRIC
Must be a soft jersey.

FABRIC WIDTH
102 cm or 122 cm.

FABRIC LENGTH
Approximately 130 cm × 112 cm for sizes 10, 12 and 14.

PATTERN
No pattern required. Measurements given include seam allowances.

TRIMMINGS
None.

CUTTING OUT
See Figures 67 to 70.

MAKING UP
See Figure 71 and Glossary of basic skills.

MEASUREMENTS REQUIRED

Figure 66
1. A–B = blouse length – in this case 56 cm.
2. C–G = neck to wrist. Use this as a check measurement to ascertain if the fabric is wide enough.
Cut a length of fabric twice the centre front length, in this case 112 cm.

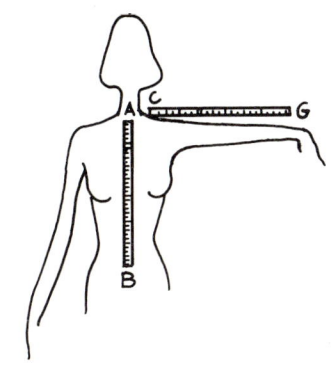

Figure 66

Figure 67
Fold the fabric in half lengthways and crossways and pin together accurately. Figure 68 shows an alternative layout for a wider fabric.

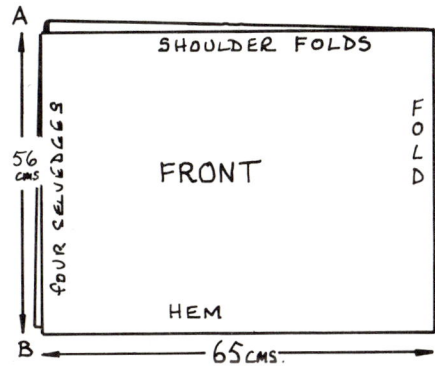

Figure 67

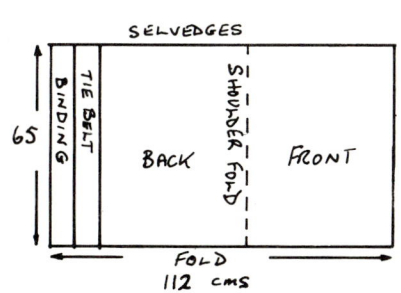

Figure 68

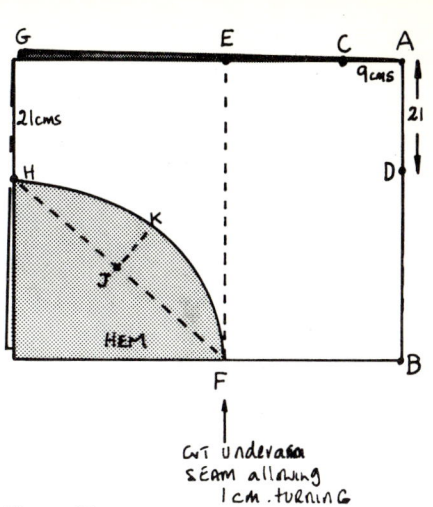

Figure 69

Figure 69
Use a tape measure and either pins or chalk to mark the following points.
A–B = centre front length.
A–C = 9 cm for front neck point.
A–D = front neck opening, 21 cm.
C–E = front shoulder, 14 cm.
E–F = draw line from E to F on the hem.
G is on the selvedge end of the fabric.
G to H is the sleeve depth (can be varied of course).
Connect F to H.
J is midway F–H.
K from J is approximately 12 cm for underarm curve.
Connect F through K to point H.
Cut from F to H, allowing a 1 cm seam.

Figure 70
Open out the fabric and carefully cut from A to C both ways and A to D. Also cut out back neck 2.5 cm.
1. With the remaining fabric cut rouleau strips to neaten neck and wrist.
2. Cut a tie belt the fabric width by 5 cm. Stitch and turn through (see Glossary of basic skills).

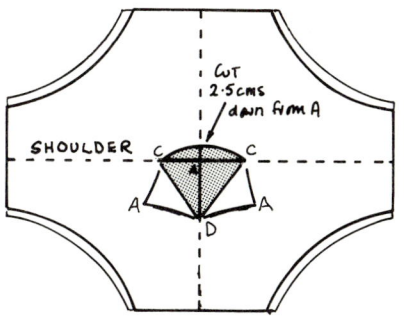

Figure 70

33

ASSEMBLY SEQUENCE

Figure 71

With garment unfolded and flat:
1. Bind neckline with prepared binding. Press.
2. Fold down and sew underarm seam 1 cm. Press.
3. Finish sleeve ends with binding (or overlocked and turned up hem).
4. Neaten hem. Press.
5. Sew belt and sew belt loops at waist.

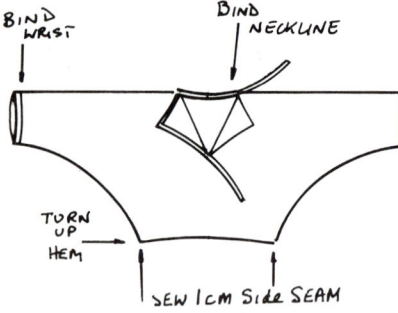

Figure 71

Style 8
Tunic dress with shoulder fastening

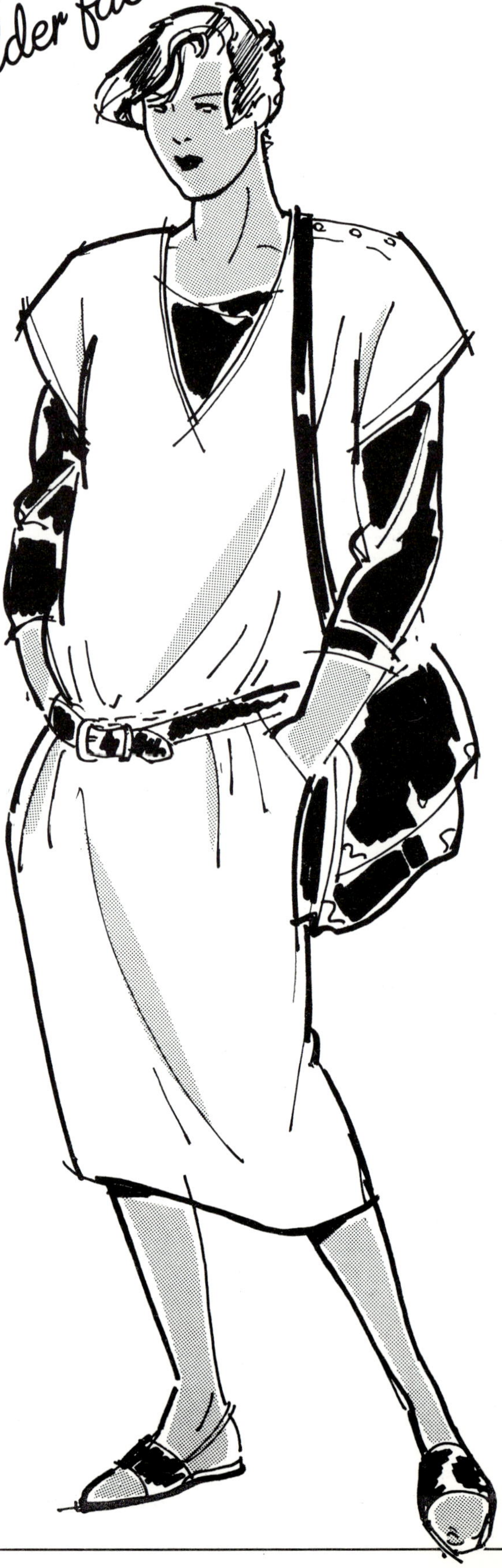

■ ★

STYLE 8

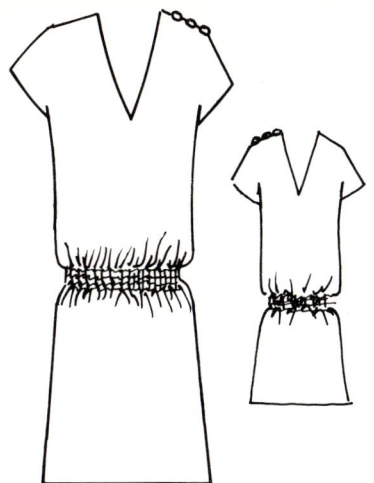

Figure 72

This style is based on a rectangle and can be cut and made simply and quickly in a variety of summer-weight fabrics.

FABRIC

To judge the fabric width, base the calculations on the hip measurement and the length from shoulder to hem approximately 1.20 cm × 90 cm for size 12.

PATTERN

This garment does not need a paper pattern. Just select the correct width fabric and cut as indicated in the diagrams. All measurements include seam allowances. Note that the wider the fabric the more gathering is required at the hip. Also the shoulder will correspondingly fall into a soft sleeve. The armhole depth could vary according to size.

TRIMMINGS

Three buttons to fasten shoulder. Elastic to draw in hip.

CUTTING OUT

See Figures 74 and 75.

MAKING UP

See assembly sequence shown in Figure 76 and Glossary of basic skills.

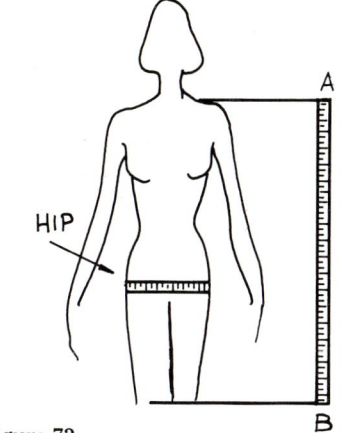

Figure 73

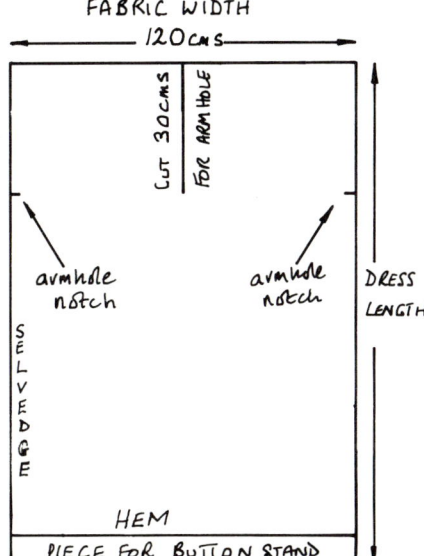

Figure 74

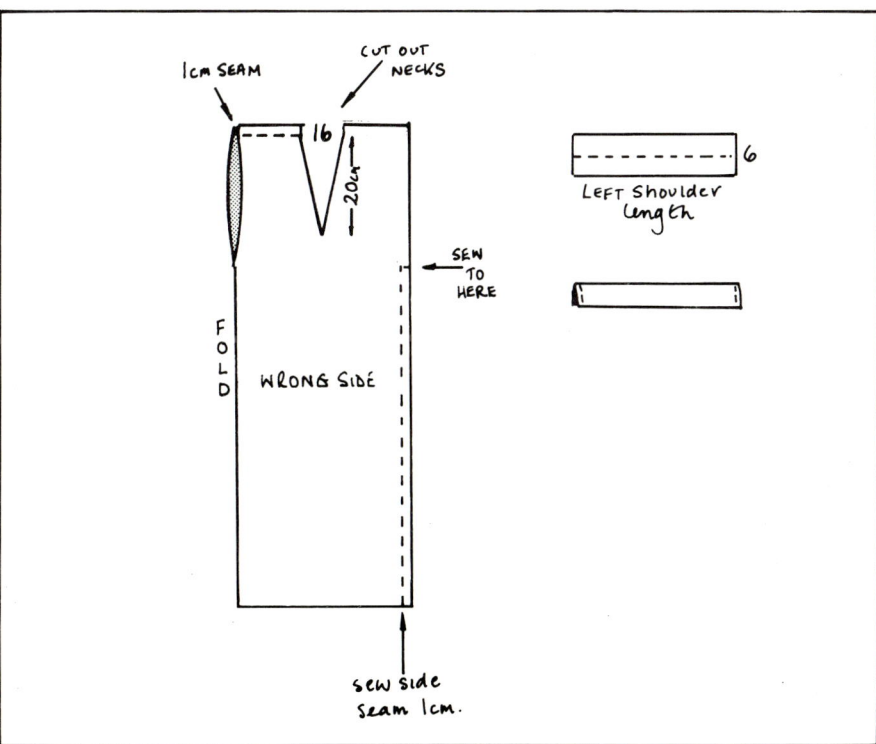

Figure 75

MEASUREMENTS REQUIRED

Figure 73

1. A to B = shoulder to required fashion length.
2. The hip measurement should be used to ensure that the fabric width is sufficient to give enough gathers.

Figure 74

Cut the fabric at least 120 cm wide by the required fashion length, in this case 90 cm, plus hem allowance of 4 cm and a piece for the button stand of 6 cm.
1. Divide the fabric in half and cut a slit 30 cm long for the right armhole.
2. Mark two notches in the selvedges 30 cm down for the left armhole.
3. Cut away button stand strip and retain.

Figure 75

1. Fold fabric in half and pin together and cut out the back and front neck together 16 cm wide × 20 cm deep.
2. Sew up right shoulder and left side seam.

Figure 76

1. Measure left shoulder and cut a strip the shoulder length by 6 cm.
2. Fold in half, sew and bag out and attach to left shoulder front.
3. Add a facing to the left back shoulder.
4. Elasticate hip.
5. Sew buttonholes into front facing.
6. Sew buttons to back left shoulder.
7. Neaten armholes and neckline by turning in 0.7 cm.
8. Overlock all seams.
9. Turn up hem 4 cm.

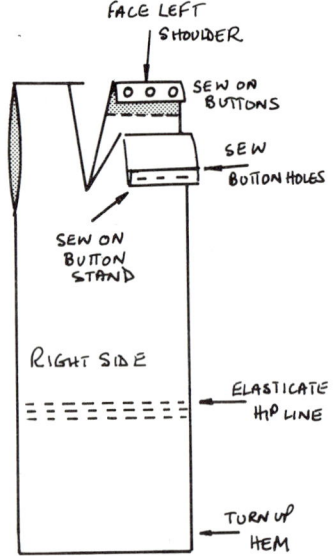

Figure 76

Style 9
Tube dress draped from the shoulder

STYLE 9

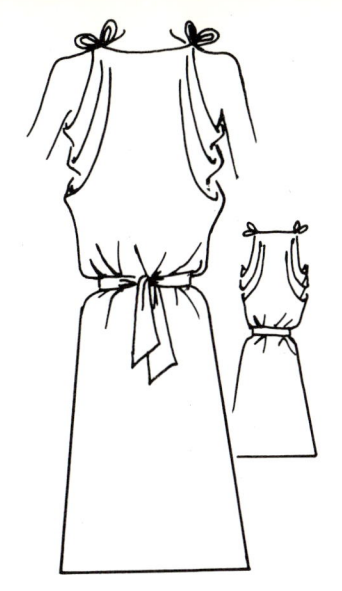

Figure 77

The following two evening dresses, which were shown to me by my friend and colleague Janet Ward, are all developed from the basic rectangle which is used simply as a tube and draped on to the figure. By varying the drape points on the body very different effects can be achieved with little skill and effort.
The dress shown in Style 9 drapes from the shoulder area and forms very soft drapes under the arms.

FABRIC

This dress must be cut in jersey for it to drape effectively. The minimum width of fabric for this style is 150 cm, as it must be full enough to drape from the shoulders and obviously fit around the hips. 150 cm will fit most sizes.

FABRIC LENGTH

The garment length, i.e. from shoulder to hem, plus enough fabric for a tie belt (see Figure 79). Seam allowances are included in the meterage stated.

PATTERN

A pattern is not needed for these styles – all measurements include seam allowances.

TRIMMINGS

None.

CUTTING OUT

See Figure 79.

MAKING UP

See sequence of assembly in Figure 80 and Glossary of basic skills.

MEASUREMENTS REQUIRED

Figure 78
1. A–B = dress length.
2. The hip measurement.

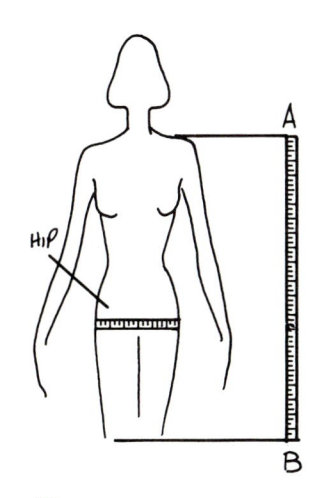

Figure 78

Figure 79
1. Lay out a length of jersey fabric. The dress length plus 10 cm for the tie belt is needed.
2. Cut off the tie belt and retain.

Figure 80
1. Fold into a tube and sew side seam.
2. Neaten around the top of the tube and then sew 2 cm down as indicated (this measurement will vary according to the size of the wearer).
3. Turn up hem.

4. A button or tie fastening can be sewn on to points C and D if desired to cover stitching.
5. Stitch and turn out the tie belt (see Glossary of basic skills page 77) and tie either around the hip or waist as desired.

Figure 79

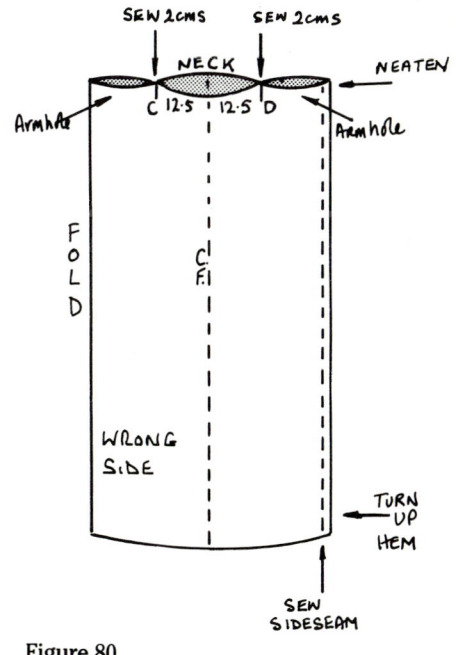

Figure 80

Style 10
Tube dress draped from above the bust

STYLE 10

Figure 81

This evening dress is supported by shoulder straps and forms beautiful soft folds under the arms. The cutting and making skills needed to produce an expensive-looking dress like this are minimal.

FABRIC

This evening dress must be cut in jersey for it to drape properly. This style is slightly more fitted than Style 9, so a narrower fabric could be used, such as 122 cm.

FABRIC LENGTH

Garment length, i.e. from neckline to hem.

PATTERN

A pattern is not needed for this style. All measurements include seam allowances.

TRIMMINGS

None

CUTTING OUT

See Figure 83.

MAKING UP

See assembly sequence in Figure 84 and Glossary of basic skills.

MEASUREMENTS REQUIRED

Figure 82
1. A–B = dress length.
2. The hip is required as a check measurement.

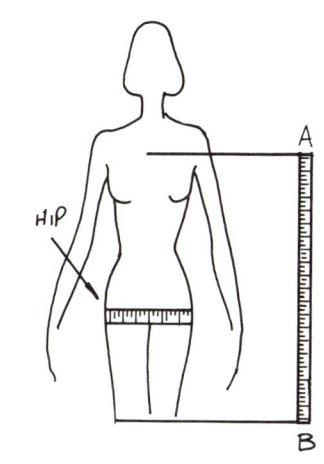

Figure 82

Figure 83
Cut a length of jersey the dress length by the fabric width. Cut off the tie and retain.

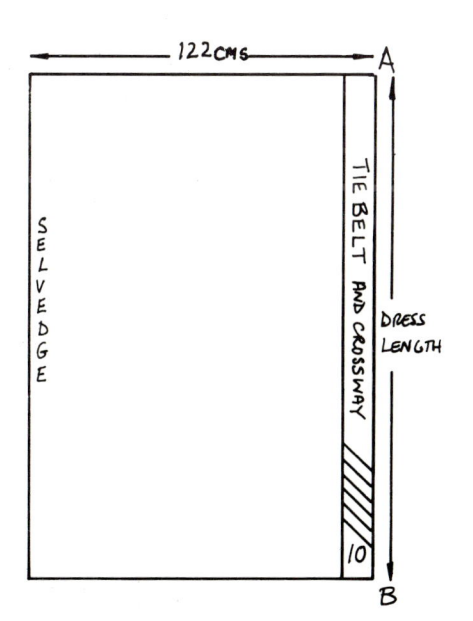

Figure 83

Figure 84
1. Cut rectangle as shown.
2. Fold into a tube and sew along selvedges for the side seam.
3. Neaten around the top of the tube and sew shoulder straps (which may be crossway strips or contrast if required) into position. The dimensions shown, i.e. 20 cm wide at neck, may be altered if desired, depending on size.
4. Turn up hem.
5. Stitch and turn out belt (see Glossary of basic skills page 77).

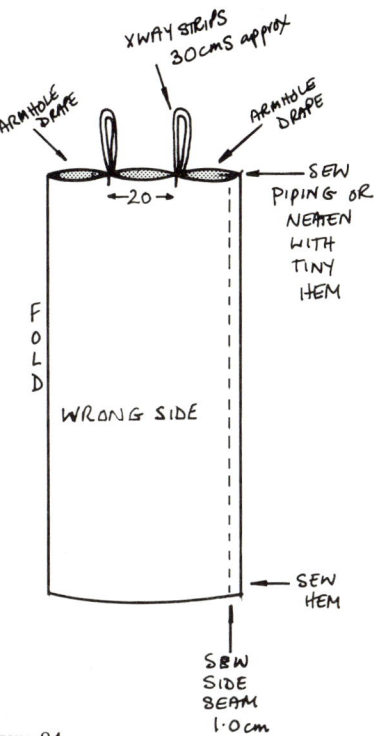

Figure 84

Style 11
Kaftan

STYLE 11

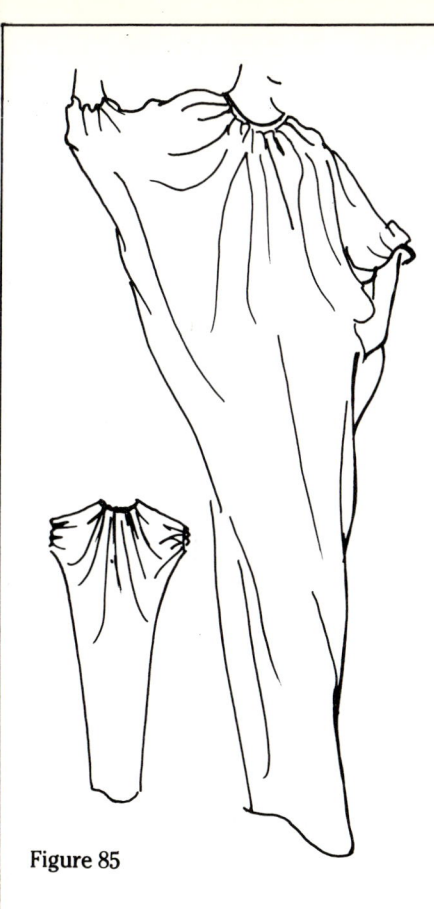

Figure 85

This kaftan-style dress has easy elegance and is softly gathered from the neck and wrist.

FABRIC

Any wide soft fabric, preferably knitted, and 150 cm or more in width.

FABRIC LENGTH

Twice the length from nape to ankle × wrist to wrist, e.g. 300 cm × 150 cm to include seams.

PATTERN

A pattern is not required for this kaftan.

TRIMMINGS

None.

CUTTING OUT

See Figures 87–89.

MAKING UP

See assembly sequence and Figure 90 and Glossary of basic skills.

MEASUREMENTS REQUIRED

Figure 86
1. Measure from A–B = wrist to wrist.
2. Measure from C–D = neck to ankle.
3. Measure around head E–F to establish size of neck opening.

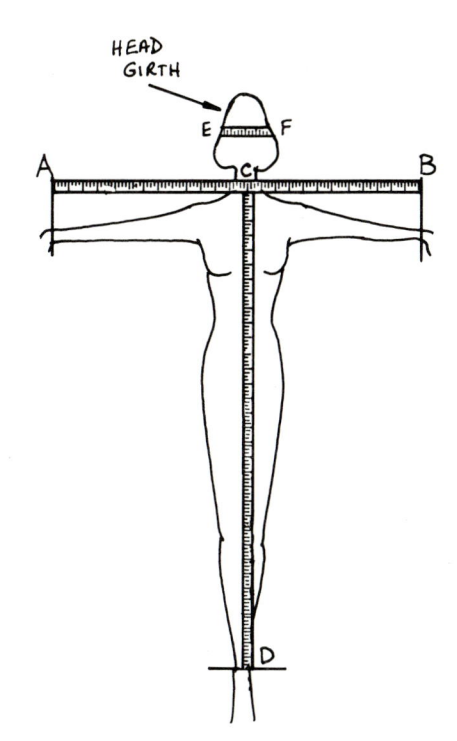

Figure 86

Figure 87
Cut a length of fabric twice the length C–D, i.e. from neck to ankle by two.
In this case:

$$147 \times 2 = 294 \text{ cm}$$
plus hem allowance 6 cm
$$\overline{}$$
300 cm

Figure 88
Fold the fabric in half and pin selvedges together.

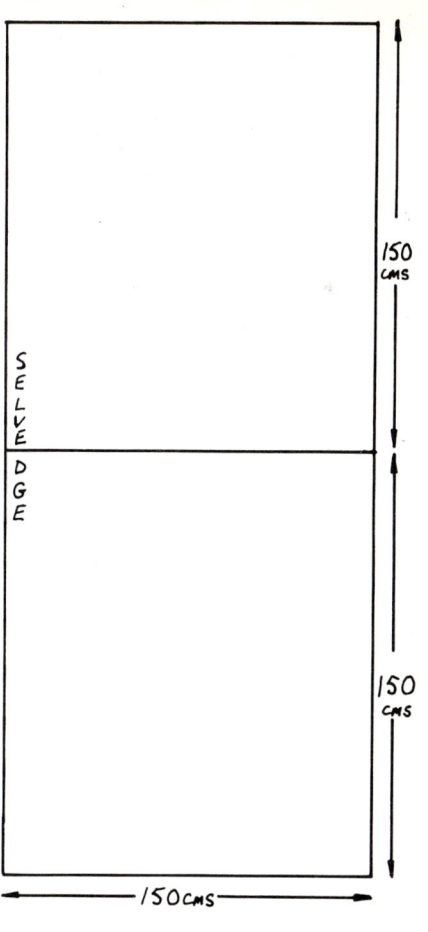

Figure 87

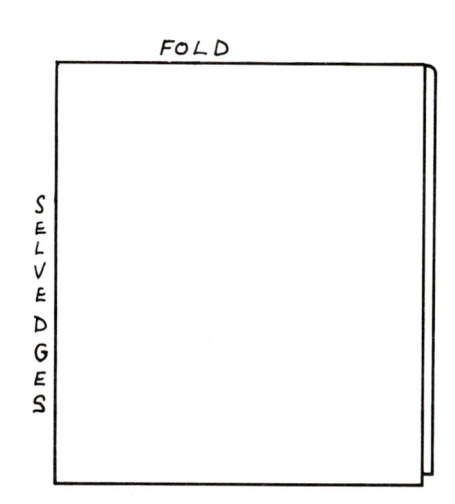

Figure 88

Figure 89
1. Fold fabric in half again lengthways and pin securely.
2. Cut out the neckline 25 cm wide by 3 cm deep.
3. Shape the side as shown in Figure 89. Carefully pin the four sections together before cutting out.
4. Cut out crossways to bind the neckline.

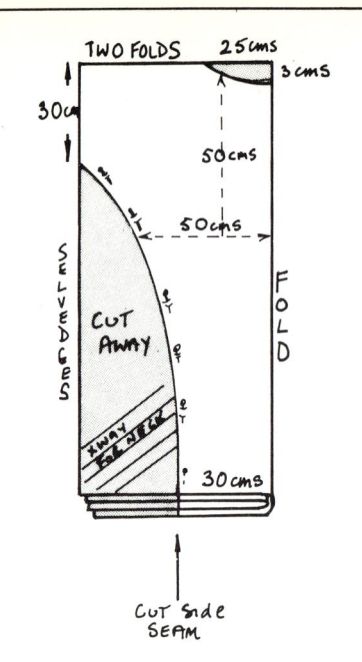

Figure 89

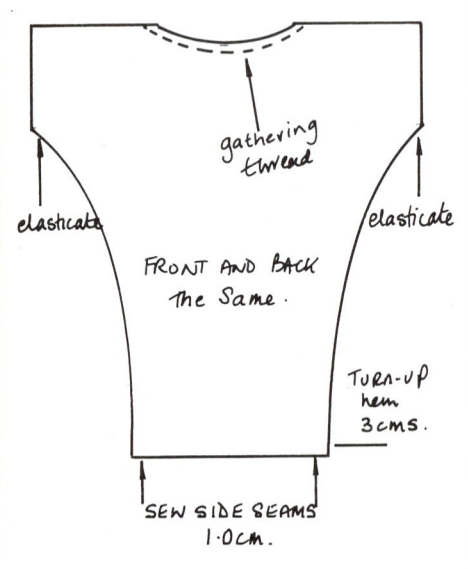

Figure 90

Style 12
Day dress

■▲★★

Figure 90
1. Open out the fabric.
2. Sew side seams.
3. Neaten neck and armholes with a rolled seam.
4. Gather up neckline to the required measurement, large enough to pull over the head. See page 75.
5. Sew on binding to the neck. See page 73.
6. Elasticate wrists.
7. Turn up hem.
8. Press.

STYLE 12

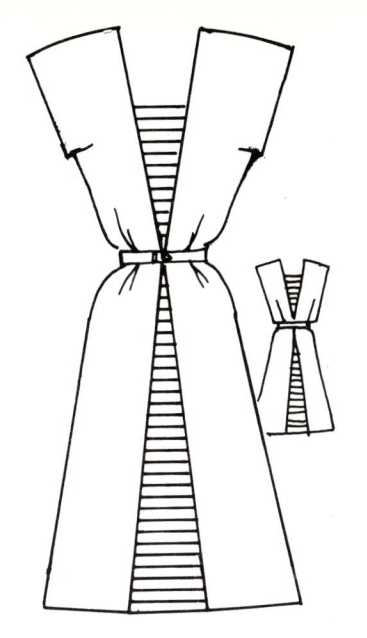

Figure 91

This day dress is cut from rectangles and triangles and the dimensions are based on the measurements of the body. It will look attractive in almost any soft fabric, such as jersey, crêpe, fine wool or cotton. The rectangles form a short sleeve and with the inset godets cut in a stripe or contrast fabric form a very pleasing effect.

FABRIC

Jersey, crêpe etc.

FABRIC LENGTH

Based on 122 cm wide wool, 120 cm is sufficient for sizes 12, 14 and 16.
Contrast: 70 cm all sizes.

PATTERN

Plan this style on to paper and add seam allowances. See page 75.

CUTTING OUT

See Figures 98 and 99.

MAKING UP

See assembly sequence and Figure 100 and Glossary of basic skills, page 75.

MEASUREMENTS REQUIRED

Figure 92

1. A–B = neckline to waist.
2. B–K = waistline to hem.
3. Neckline depth.
4. Half waist measurement.
5. Half top hip measurement (10 cm down from waist).

In this example the following measurements are used.
1. A–B = 43 cm.
2. B–K = 60 cm plus 4 cm for the hem.
3. Neckline depth 18 cm.
4. Half waist measurement plus 2.5 cm ease = 35 cm.
5. Top hip 82 cm plus 4 cm ease.

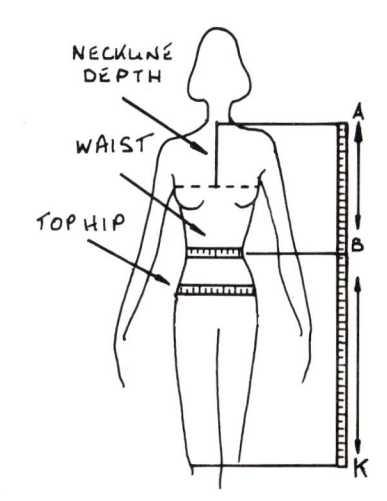

Figure 92

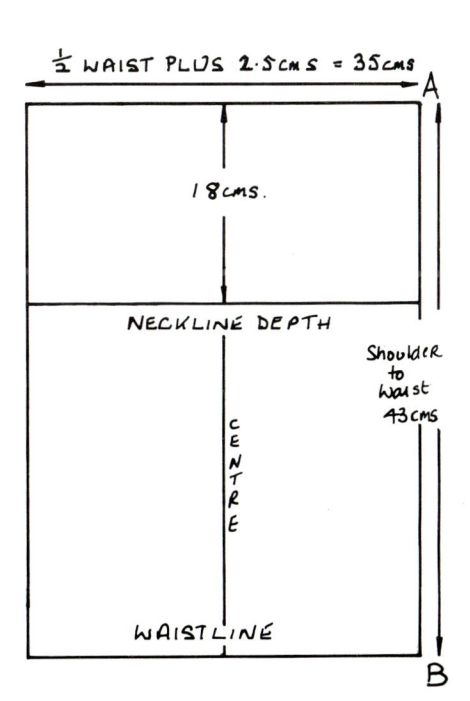

Figure 93 *Bodice*

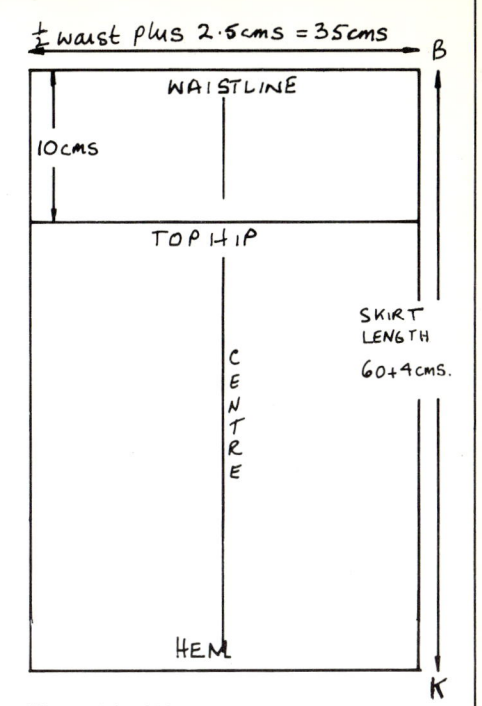

Figure 94 *Skirt*

Figure 93
The bodice:
Draw a rectangle as shown 35 cm × 43 cm. Mark neckline depth.

Figure 94
Draw a rectangle as shown 35 cm × 64 cm. Mark top hip.

Note The bodice and skirt are based upon the waist measurement. The wider parts of the body at bust and top hip are obtained by inserting a triangle which makes up the difference between bust and hip and waist.

Figure 95

1. Mark points A–B–C–D.
2. Draw the triangle as shown. E and F are 7 cm from point G (located on the centre line). This triangle when inserted into line C–D increases the measurement to 49 cm which is half the bust measurement.
3. Mark armhole depth 22 cm down from A.
4. Trace-off A–B–D–G–C–A and add 1 cm allowances all around and cut four times – two for the front and two for the back.
5. Trace-off gusset E–G–F–D and add 1 cm seam allowances.

43

STYLE 12

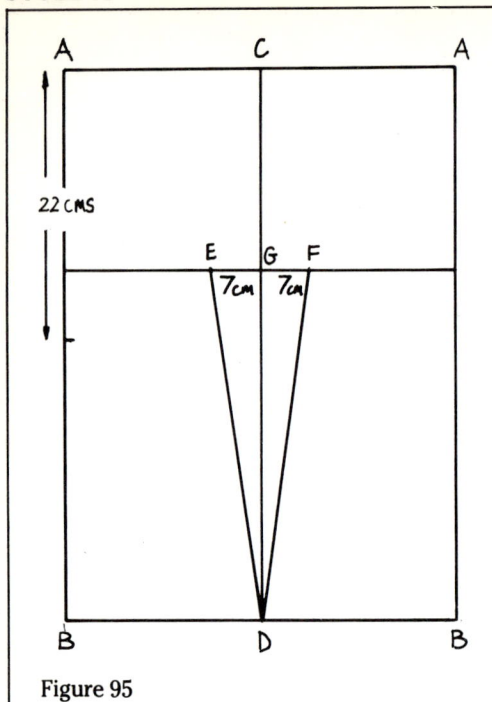

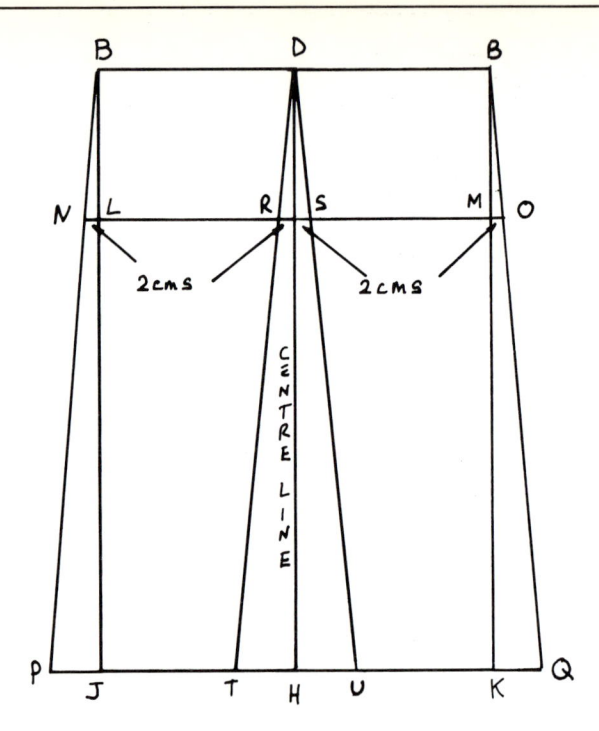

Figure 95

Figure 96

Figure 96
1. Extend line L and M 2 cm.
2. R and S are 2 cm from the skirt centre line.
Connect B through N to locate P on extended line J–P. Repeat B–O–Q on the other side.
3. Trace-off B–N–P–H–D–B and add 1 cm seam allowances and cut four times in fabric, two for the front and two for the back.
4. Trace off gusset D–S–U–H–T–R–D and cut two.

Figure 97
This shows the finished pattern shapes.

Figure 98
This shows the fabric layout for the plain jersey.

Figure 99
This shows the fabric layout for the striped jersey.

Figure 97

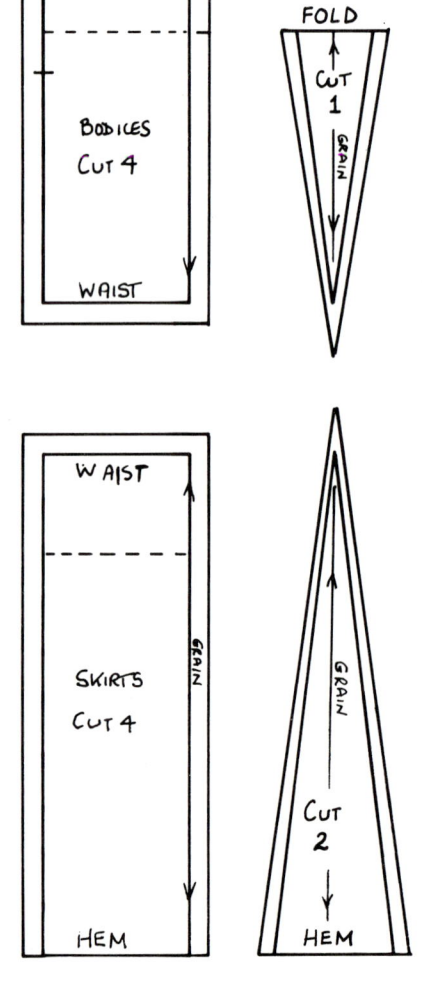

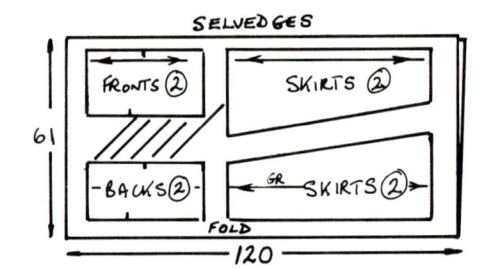

Figure 98

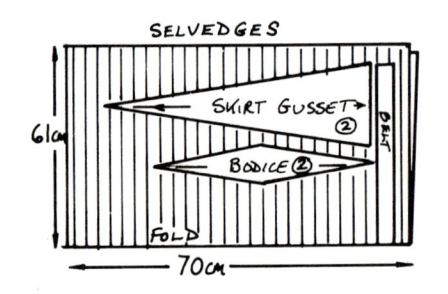

Figure 99

STYLE 12

ASSEMBLY SEQUENCE

Figure 100

1. Fold front and back vest in half lengthways and either overlock or sew edges together to hold firmly.
2. Taking a 1 cm seam sew vests into the back and front bodice sections.
3. Neaten back and front skirt gussets and sew into the back and front skirt sections.
4. Join front bodice waist to the front skirt waist and neaten seam.
5. Join the back bodice waist to the back skirt waist and neaten seams.
6. With the garment inside out, join the front to the back by sewing up the shoulder seams.
7. Sew up the skirt side seams and underarm seams and insert zip (see page 78).
8. Bind or pipe the neckline.
9. Neaten the armhole with a 1 cm turning.
10. Turn up skirt hem.
11. Sew up belt (see page 78).
12. Press.

Figure 101

The garment will look the same back and front.

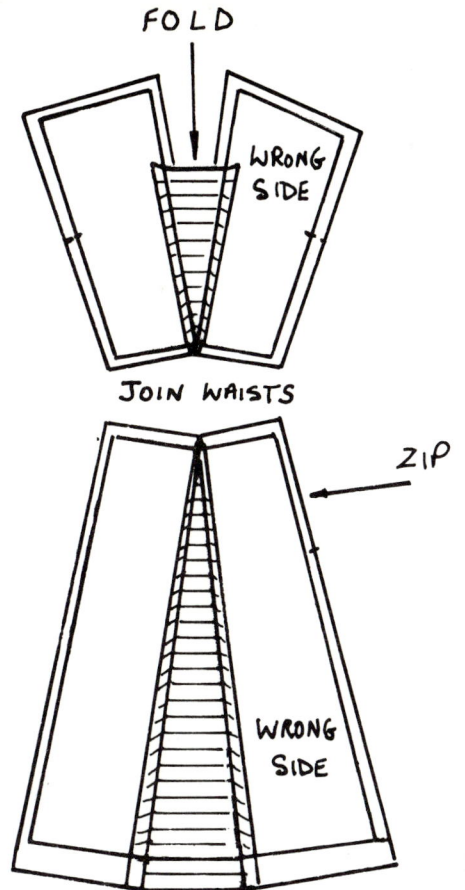

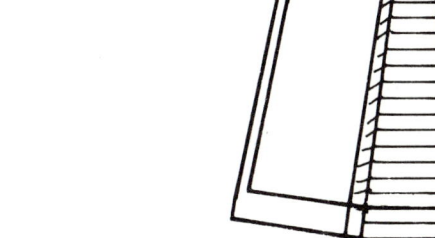

Figure 100

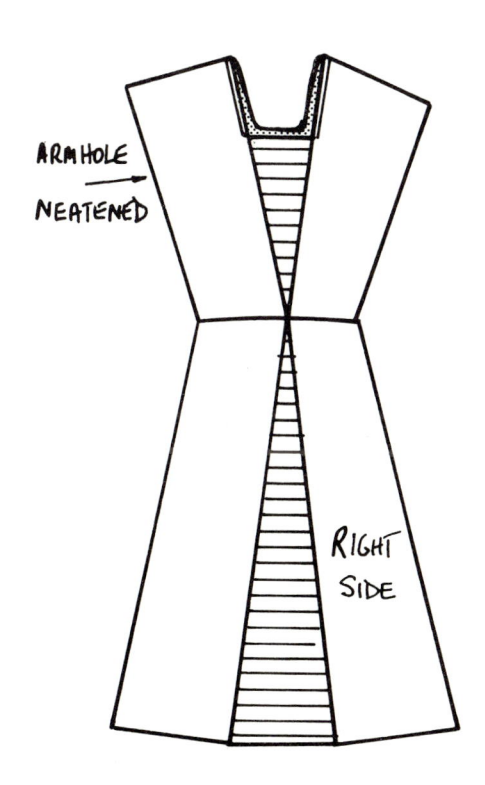

Figure 101

Style 13
Full circle skirt

STYLE 13

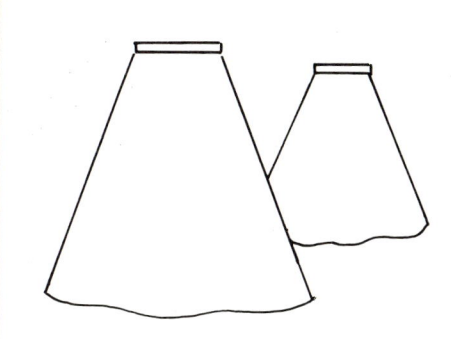

Figure 102

The full circle skirt is easy and comfortable to wear and is suitable for all seasons. It is very easy to cut and sew and will hang well in almost any fabric.

FABRIC

Must be wide enough to accommodate the length of the skirt plus the waist curve. See Figures 105 and 106.

FABRIC LENGTH

As an example, a full circle skirt to fit 66 cm waist and with a finished length of 60 cm will require 150 cm × 150 cm.

PATTERN

Mark the skirt outline directly on to the fabric.

TRIMMINGS

One 17 cm zip and interlining for the waist band.

CUTTING OUT

See Figures 104–6 and 108.

MAKING UP

See assembly sequence and Glossary of basic skills.

MEASUREMENTS REQUIRED

Figure 103

1. Waist girth (taken with the tape measure held tightly).
2. Required skirt length (A–B) from waist to hem, plus 1.5 cm for the hem allowance.
3. For this example the waist will be 65 cm plus 1 cm tolerance = 66 cm.
4. Waist to hem, A–B, will be 60 cm in this example plus 1.5 cm for the hem = 61.5 cm.

This skirt comprises two sections and is joined at the side seams. Start by cutting the fabric into two lengths of 75 cm.

Figure 103

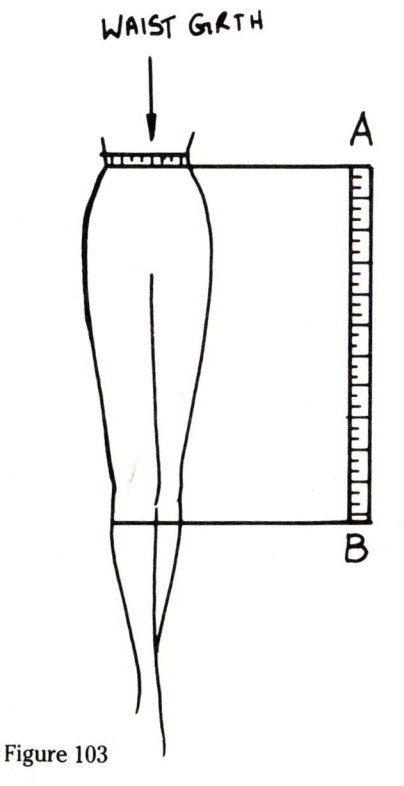

Figure 104

Fold one length of fabric accurately and pin the selvedges together.

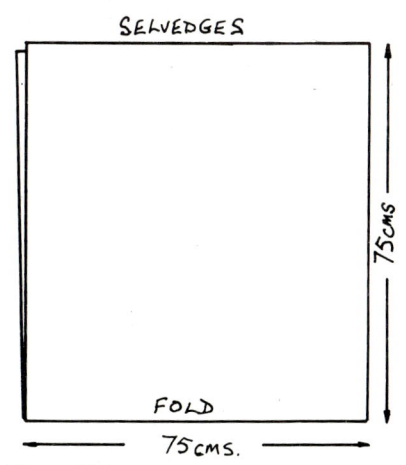

Figure 104

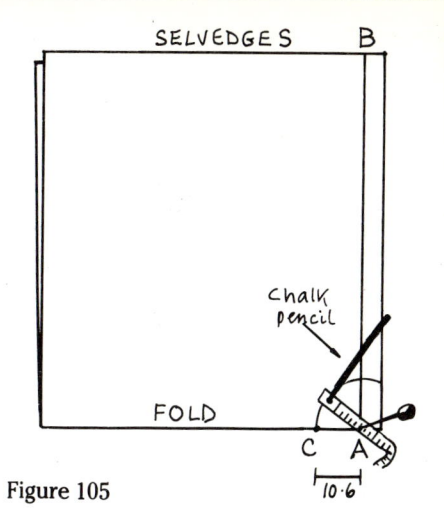

Figure 105

1. Using chalk or a chalk pencil draw line A–B which is 2 cm in from the fabric edge
2. Calculate the radius of the waist, i.e. the waist measurement minus 2.5 cm divided by 6. In this example:
   (a) 66 cm − 2.5 cm = 63.5 cm.
   (b) 63.5 cm ÷ 6 cm = 10.58 cm.
   (c) 10.58 cm is rounded up to 10.6 cm.
   (d) 10.6 cm = the radius of the waist.
3. Measure 10.6 cm down from A and mark point C with chalk. Place the chalk pencil into the hole at the end of the tape measure and position on to point C. Also place a bradawl into the appropriate measurement and spike on to point A. Swing the arc firmly holding the tape measure taut at both points.

Figure 106

1. Measure 61.5 cm down on the fold to establish point D.
2. Using the same tape measure technique swing an arc through point D for the hemline.

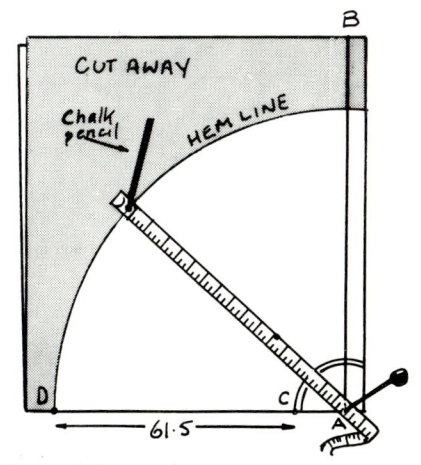

Figure 106

47

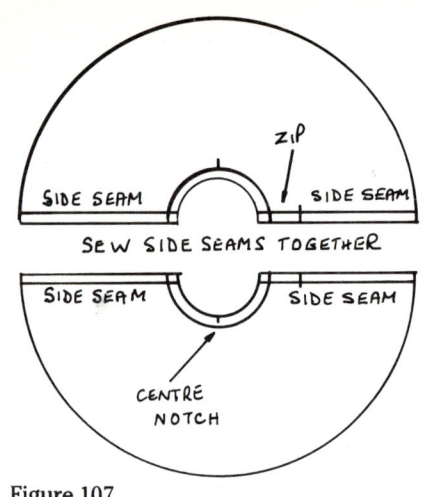

Figure 107

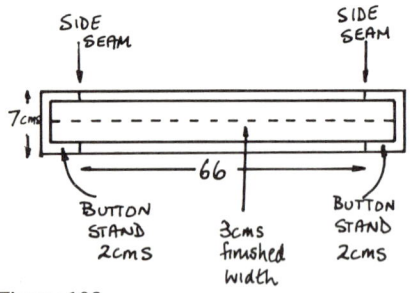

Figure 108

3. Add 1 cm seam allowance at the waist (also by the arc method).
4. Cut out skirt.

Fold another length of fabric. Lay the cut skirt on to it, pin accurately and cut out another skirt.

Figure 107
Shows the two skirt sections and the zip position.

Figure 108
Cut the waistband from the remaining fabric 70 cm × 7 cm. Cut an interlining 70 cm × 4 cm.

ASSEMBLY SEQUENCE

1. Sew side seams leaving an opening of 18 cm at the left side for the zip.
2. Insert the zip (see Glossary of basic skills, page 78).
3. Assemble waistband (see Glossary of basic skills, page 77).
4. Insert waistband.
5. Hang skirt overnight and see if the skirt has dropped. If it has, level the skirt.
6. Turn up hem.
7. Press.

Style 14
Half circle skirt

STYLE 14

Figure 109

The half circle skirt is another attractive garment which is easy to cut and sew. It will also look good in a variety of fabrics.

FABRIC

Almost any soft fabric will be suitable.

FABRIC LENGTH

So that this skirt can be cut in one piece, the fabric is folded selvedge way. This allows skirts of various lengths to fit into the fabric. Select a fabric about 115 cm wide. This will allow the skirt length to be adjusted as required. The skirt will need approximately 2 m.

PATTERN

Directly on to the fabric.

TRIMMINGS

Zip for CB opening.

CUTTING OUT

See Figures 112 –14 and 116.

MAKING UP

See assembly sequence and Glossary of basic skills.

MEASUREMENTS REQUIRED

Figure 110
1. Waist girth (taken with the tape measure held firmly).
2. Required skirt length (A–B) from waist to hem plus 1.5 cm for the hem allowance.
3. For this example the waist will be 65 cm plus 1 cm tolerance = 66 cm.
4. The skirt length will be 76 cm plus 1.5 cm = 77.5 cm.

Note This skirt is usually cut in one piece and is seamed at the side. Cut a length of fabric 95 cm × 90 cm.

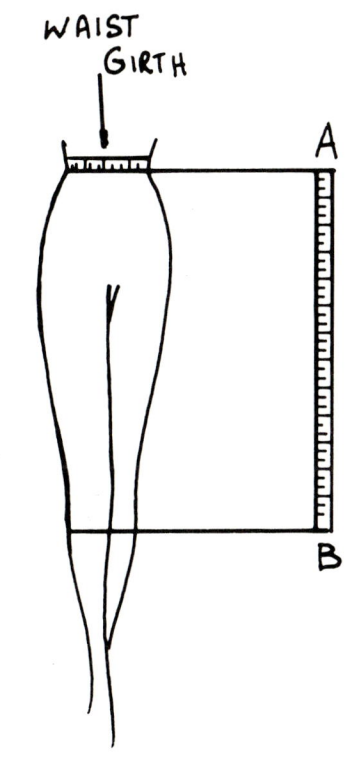

Figure 110

Figure 111
Fold the fabric lengthways and pin the selvedges together.

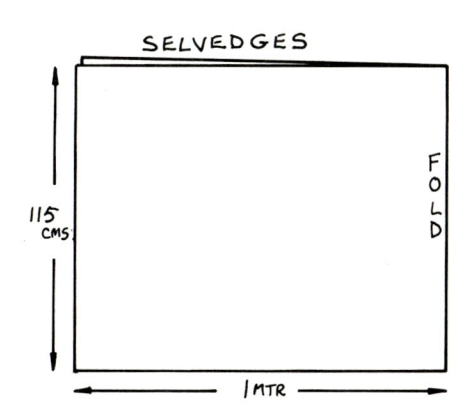

Figure 111

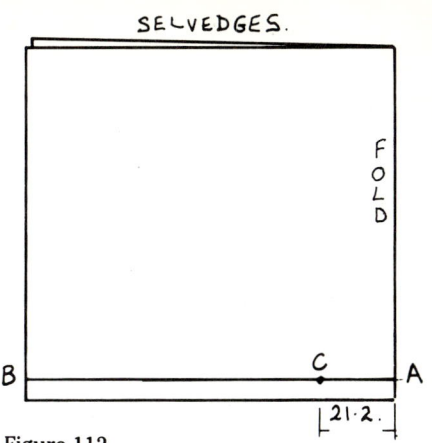

Figure 112

Figure 112
1. Using a chalk pencil draw line A–B which is 2 cm in from the fabric edge.
2. Calculate the waist radius by taking waist measurement minus 2.5 cm divided by 3. In this example: 66 cm − 2.5 cm = 63.5 cm.
63.5 cm ÷ 3 = 21.2 cm waist radius.
3. Measure 21.2 cm down from A and mark point C.

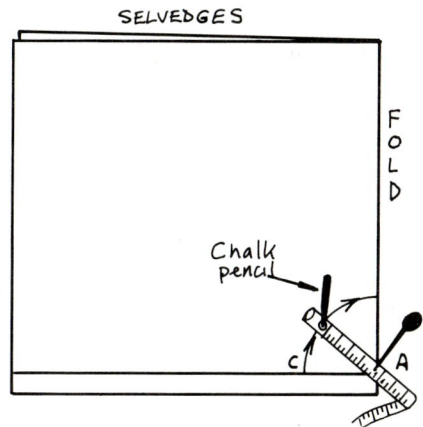

Figure 113

Figure 113
Place the chalk pencil into the hole at the end of a tape measure and position point of pencil on to point C. Place a bradawl into the appropriate measurement and spike through the tape measure on to point A. Swing an arc firmly holding the tape measure taut at both points, marking the waist with the chalk.

49

STYLE 14

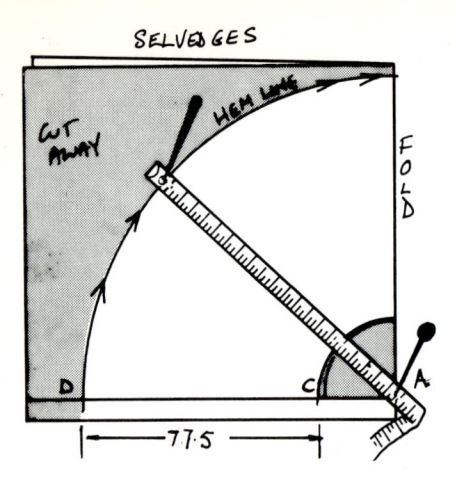

Figure 114

Figure 114
1. Measure down from C the skirt length 77.5 cm. Using the tape measure technique swing an arc through point D from the pivot point A for the hemline.
2. Add 1 cm seam allowance at the waist (also by the arc method).
3. Cut out the skirt.

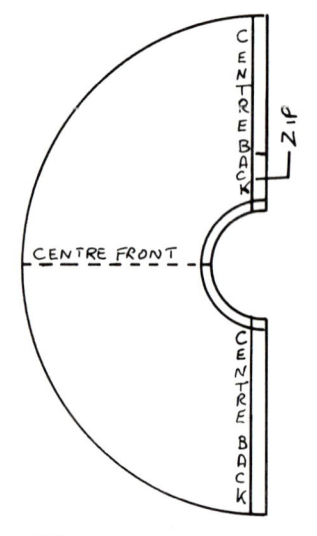

Figure 115

Figure 115
Shows the cut out skirt.

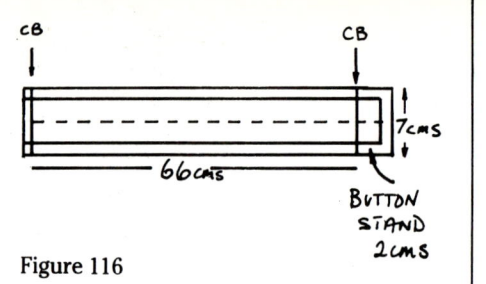

Figure 116

Figure 116
Using the spare fabric cut out a waistband 70 cm × 7 cm. Also cut interlining 70 cm × 4 cm.

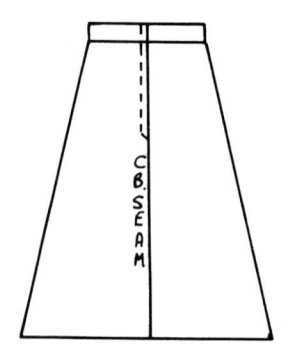

Figure 117

Figure 117
Skirt showing CB seam and zip position.

ASSEMBLY SEQUENCE

1. Sew centre back seam leaving an opening of 18 cm for the zip.
2. Insert the zip.
3. Assemble waistband (see Glossary of basic skills, page 77).
4. Sew on waistband.
5. Hang skirt overnight to enable the skirt to drop.
6. Level the skirt.
7. Turn up the hem.

Style 15
A-line skirt

STYLE 15

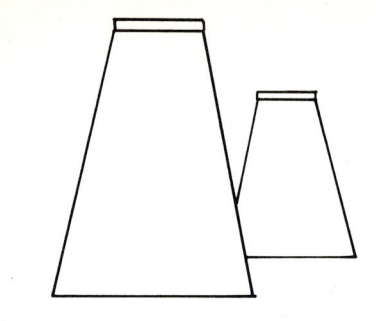

Figure 118

The traditional A-line shape is based on the relationship between the waist and hip measurement. It makes an ideal shaped skirt for adult or child.

FABRIC

Any lightish weight fabric will be suitable.

FABRIC LENGTH

This will depend on fabric width and individual size. As an example, the size cut in this style will take approximately 80 cm × 122 cm for a fabric without a nap. See fabric chart.

PATTERN

A pattern is needed for this style.

TRIMMINGS

18 cm zip.

CUTTING OUT

See Figure 129.

MAKING UP

See assembly sequence, Figure 130 and Glossary of basic skills.

MEASUREMENTS REQUIRED

Figure 119

1. A–B = the top hip measurement taken approximately 10 cm down from the waist. The tape measurement should not be held too tight when measuring.
2. The waist measurement, taken firmly.
3. A–C = the required skirt length. The measurements used for this style are as follows:
66 cm waist plus 2 cm tolerance = 68 cm
84 cm top hip plus 2 cm tolerance = 86 cm
66 cm length plus 4 cm for the hem = 70 cm

Start by dividing the waist and top hip measurement by 8:
68 ÷ 8 = 8.5 cm (= one-eighth of waist)
86 ÷ 8 = 10.7 cm (= one-eighth of top hip)

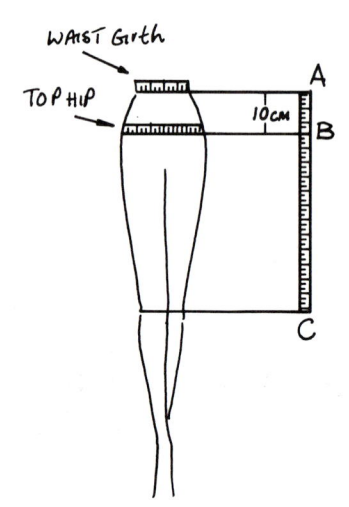

Figure 119

Figure 120

Fold a large sheet in half, lengthways (it must be at least 30 cm longer than the skirt length to establish the pivot point).

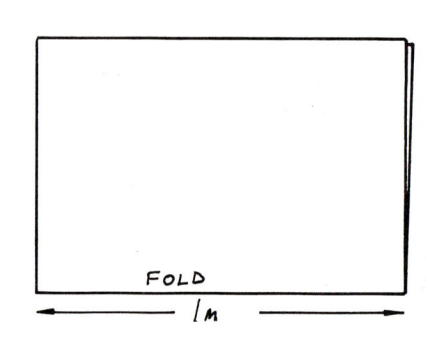

Figure 120

Figure 121

1. Draw line A–A which will equal one-eighth of the waist, e.g. 8.5 cm.
2. Draw line B–B which will equal one-eighth of the top hip.
3. Draw line C–A for the skirt length.

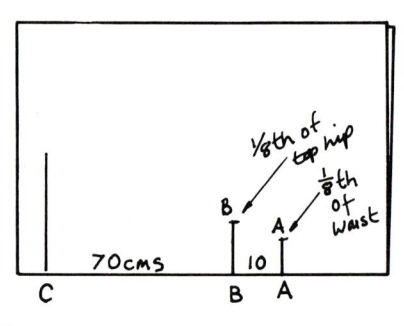

Figure 121

Figure 122

Connect points A–B with a line to locate point D at the hem and E on the paper fold.
Three arcs are needed, so use a tape measure, pencil and a bradawl as illustrated in Figure 123.

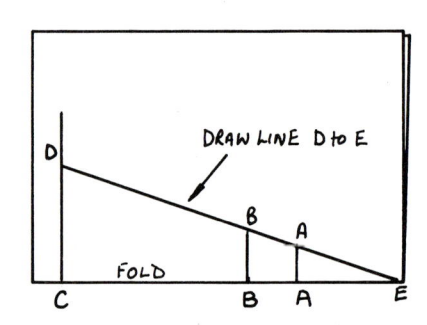

Figure 122

Figure 123

1. Using E as a pivot, swing an arc through point A with the pencil held tautly.
2. Again, using E as a pivot, swing an arc through point B.
3. Using E as a pivot, swing an arc through point C. Add a 1.5 cm turning for the waistline. See Figure 124.

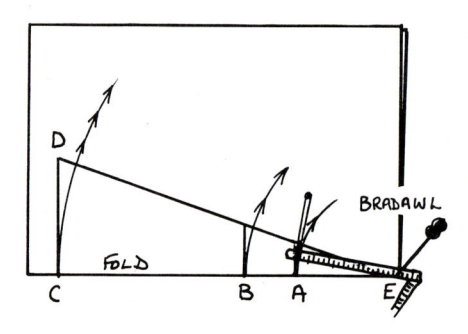

Figure 123

STYLE 15

Figure 124
Cut from C to D and along waist seam allowance. Fold line D–E.

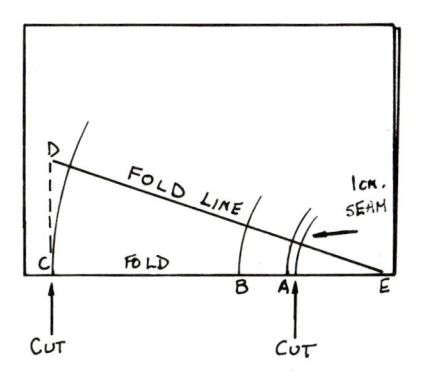

Figure 124

Figure 127

Figure 128

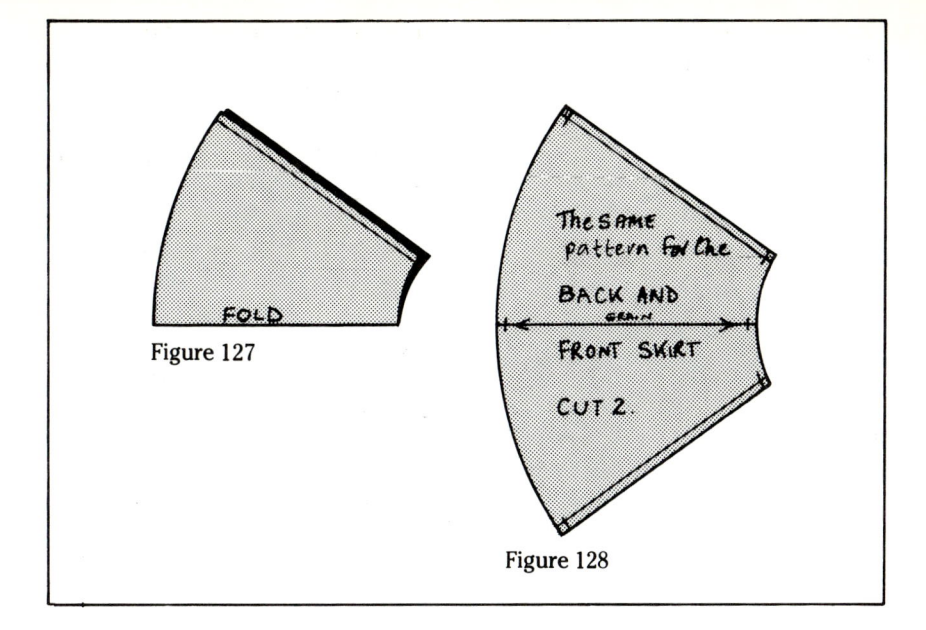

Figure 125
Fold original skirt upward, creasing firmly on the fold line (D–E). Mark points D around to C and along to A–A.

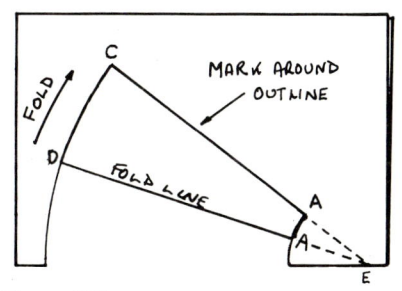

Figure 125

Figure 129
This shows the suggested cloth layout.

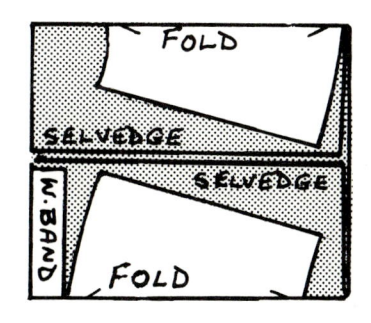

Figure 129

ASSEMBLY SEQUENCE

Figure 130
1. Sew up side seam leaving an 18 cm gap for the zip.
2. Insert the zip, see page 78.
3. Sew up other side seam.
4. Use a petersham finish for the waist (see page 77) or cut a waistband as other skirt styles.
5. Turn-up hem.
6. Press.

Figure 126
Add 1.5 cm to line C–A for the side seam.

Figure 127
Cut out complete skirt.

Figure 128
The opened out pattern: cut twice, one section for the back and one section for the front.

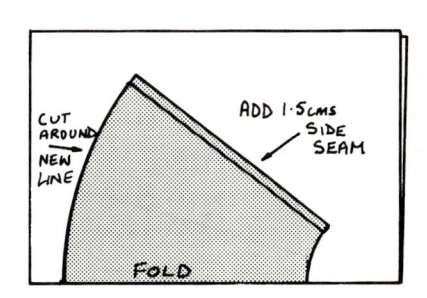

Figure 126

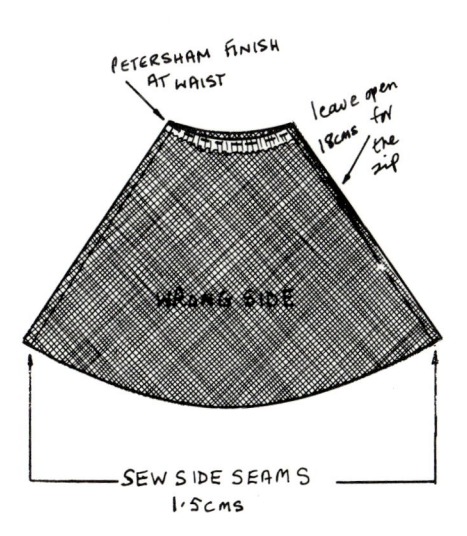

Figure 130

● ★★★

Style 16
Four-panelled spiral skirt with draped hem

STYLE 16

Figure 131

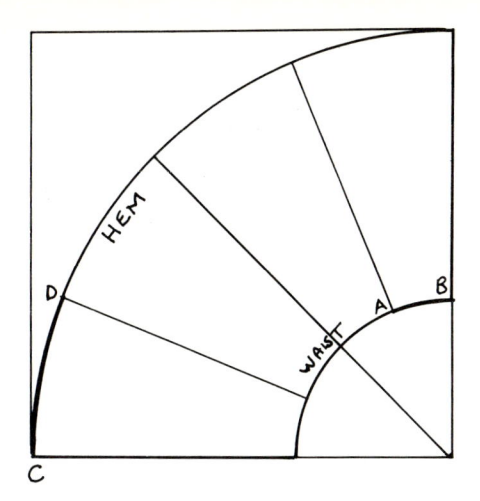

This is one of the most attractive skirts as it fits fairly snugly around the hips and gently flares into a very draped hem. It is not very easy to construct as it does require some accurate drafting and cutting. The effort, however, is well worth it, as the results look really attractive and expensive.

FABRIC

Any soft fabric will be suitable, but avoid checks and stripes. Concentrate on plain or small floral prints.

FABRIC LENGTH

Approximately 4 m × 102 cm minimum for a size 12.

PATTERN

A pattern is needed for this skirt.

TRIMMINGS

Zip, 20 cm long.

CUTTING OUT

See Figure 137.

Figure 132

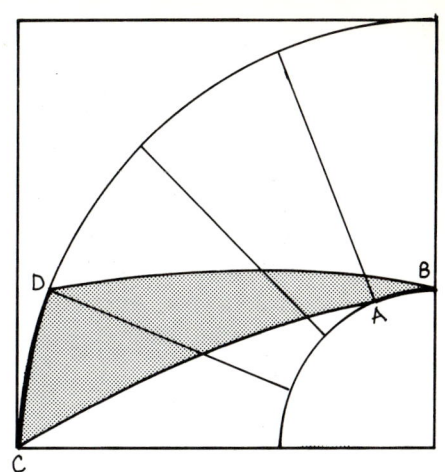

Figure 133

Figure 134

Figure 135

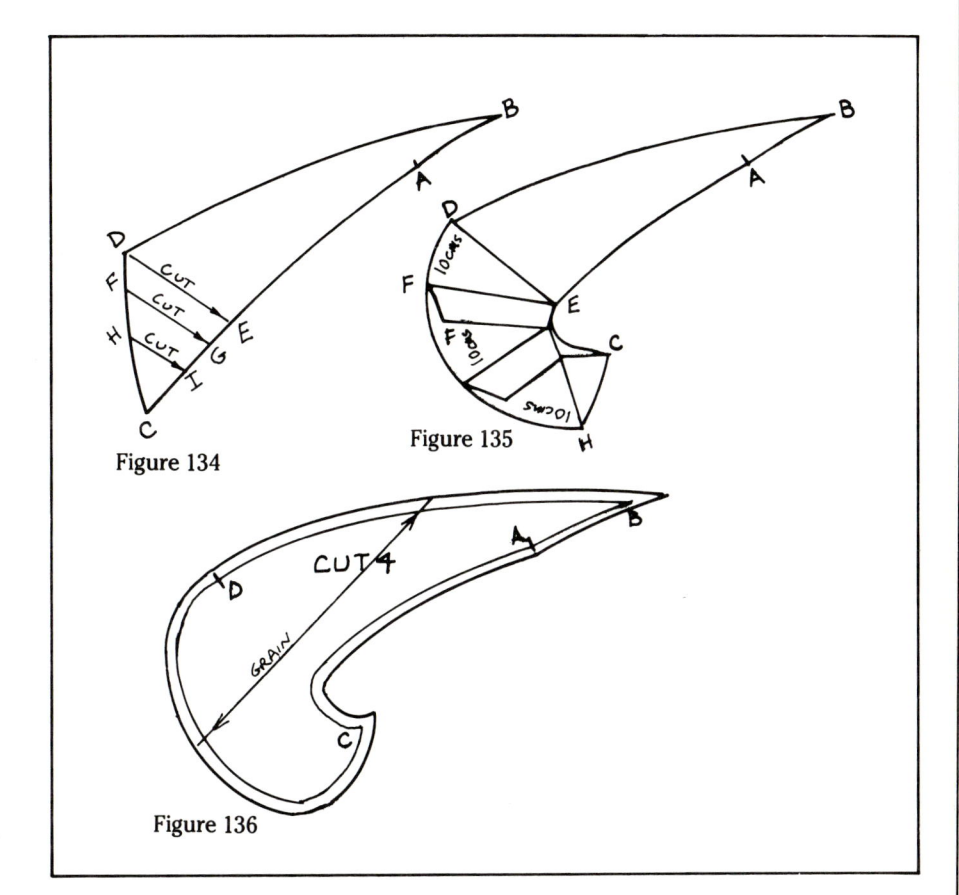

Figure 136

MAKING UP

See Figure 138 and Glossary of basic skills.
This spiral skirt is developed from Style 15 which is the A-line skirt based on the waist and top hip measurements. So begin by referring to Style 15 and construct the basic skirt from Figures 120 to 128.

Figure 132

Construct the A-line skirt pattern or reuse the previous pattern. Divide the skirt pattern into four equal sections.
A–B will equal one-quarter of the waist measurement.
C–D will equal one-quarter of the hem measurement.

Figure 133

Connect A to C with a slightly curved line. Connect B to D with the same shaped line so that lines A–C and B–D are the same length. This section is one-quarter of the complete skirt.

STYLE 16

Figures 134 and 135
To make this skirt fuller at the hem follow this procedure:
1. Cut out section A–B–D–C.
2. Draw lines D–E, F–G and H–I and cut along them – open out each section approximately 10 cm (this will depend on the length of the skirt) and lay on to another sheet of paper.
3. Curve line D to H.
4. Curve line E to C.
Note B to D must still equal A to C in length.

Figure 136

The finished pattern section:
Carefully mark point D on to the pattern and add seam allowances all around of 1 cm.

FABRIC LAYOUT

Figure 137
This will vary according to the width of fabric selected. Lay the pattern on to the fabric and mark with chalk and then repeat this four times. Cut out. If a waistband is required, cut one as in Style 15.

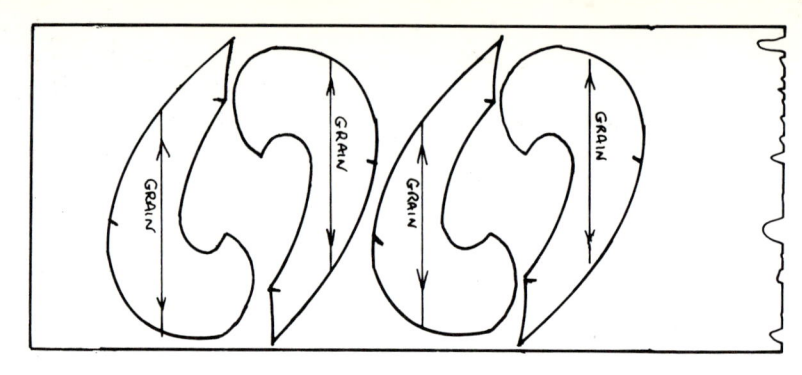

Figure 137

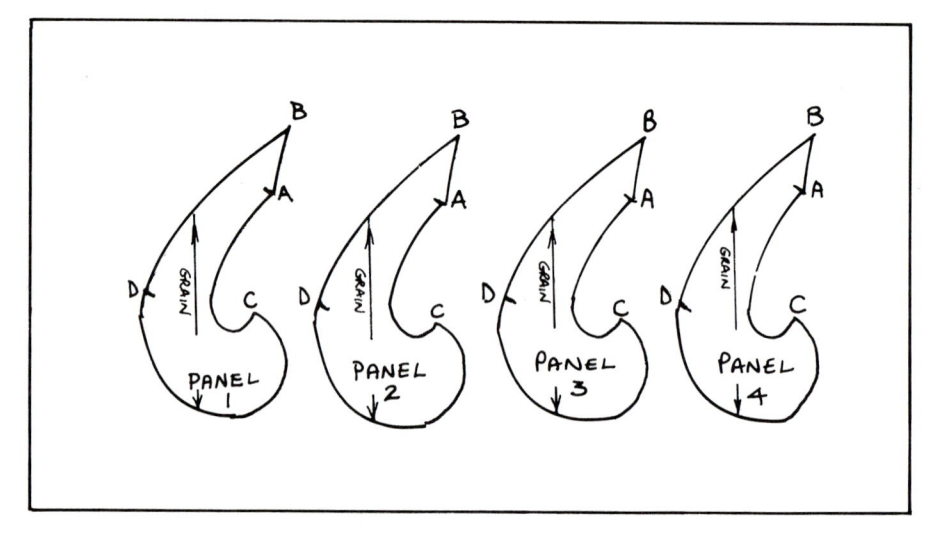

Figure 138

ASSEMBLY SEQUENCE

Figure 138
1. Sew A to C on panel 2 to B to D on panel 1.
2. Sew A to C on panel 3 to B to D on panel 2.
3. Sew A to C on panel 4 to B to D on panel 3.
4. Sew B to D on panel 4 to A to C on panel 1, leaving an opening for the zip (the sections sewn together will form a spiral). Insert zip, see Glossary of basic skills.
5. Neaten D to C on all panels as this will form the flounced hem.

Note All the A to Bs form the waist. Cut and sew on to a waistband if required or use a petersham finish. See Glossary of basic skills.

Style 17
Tablecloth skirt

STYLE 17

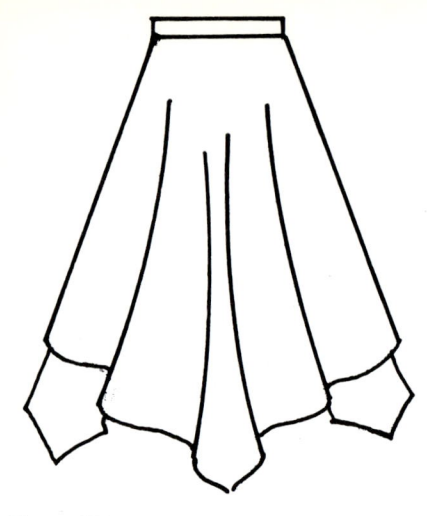

Figure 139

This interesting skirt is made of two layers of fine material and hangs from the waist into eight points.

FABRIC

Any soft fabric will be suitable for this style.

FABRIC LENGTH

This skirt could be cut with the fold along the weft. This will give a wider skirt, 310 cm × 90 cm for a skirt of 66 cm waist and 66 cm length.

PATTERN

Directly on to the fabric – no pattern required.

TRIMMINGS

Zip.

CUTTING OUT

See Figures 141–3.

MAKING UP

See Figure 144 and Glossary of basic skills.

MEASUREMENTS REQUIRED

Figure 140

1. Waist girth (taken with the tape measure held tightly).
2. Required skirt length (A–B) from waist to hem, plus 1.5 cm for the hem allowance.
3. For this example the waist will be 65 cm plus 1 cm tolerance = 66 cm.
4. Waist to hem will be 60 cm plus 1.5 cm for the hem allowance = 61.5 cm.

This skirt is made up of four sections, i.e. one layer joined at the side seam as in skirt Style 13. This is then doubled to give two layers. Start by cutting the fabric into four lengths of 75 cm each.

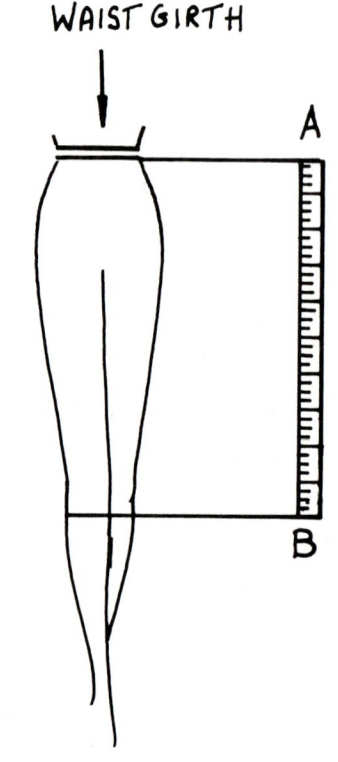

Figure 140

Figure 141

Fold one length of fabric accurately and pin the selvedges together.

Figure 142

1. Using chalk or a chalk pencil draw line A–B which is 2 cm in from the fabric edge.
2. Calculate the radius of the waist, i.e. the waist measurement minus 2.5 cm divided by 6. In this example: 66 cm − 2.5 cm = 63.5.

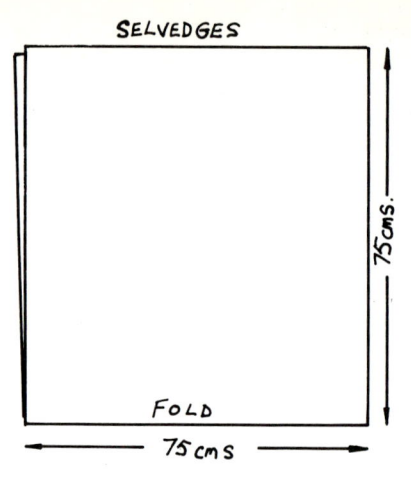

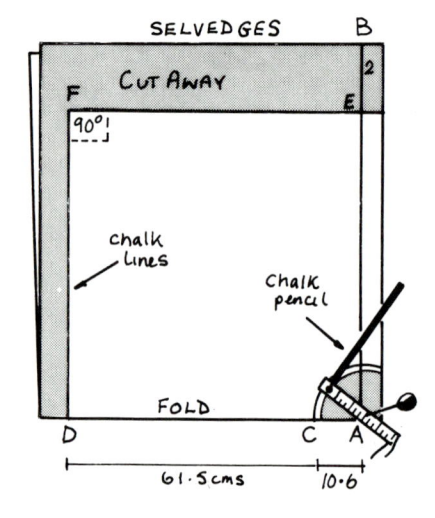

Figure 141

Figure 142

63.5 cm ÷ 6 cm = 10.58 cm. Round up to 10.6 cm. 10.6 cm equals the radius of the waist.

3. Measure 10.6 cm down from A and mark point C with chalk. Place the chalk pencil into the hole at the end of the tape measure and position on to point C. Also place a bradawl into the appropriate measurement and spike on to point A. Swing the arc firmly holding the tape measure taut at both points.
4. Add seam allowances at the waist by the same method.
5. Measure 61.5 cm down on the fold to establish point D.
6. Measure 61.5 cm up along line A–B to establish point E square both ways to establish F.
7. Cut this skirt out and repeat the procedure three times or lay three double thicknesses of fabric and lay the original on top of it.

Figure 143
This shows the four cut sections.

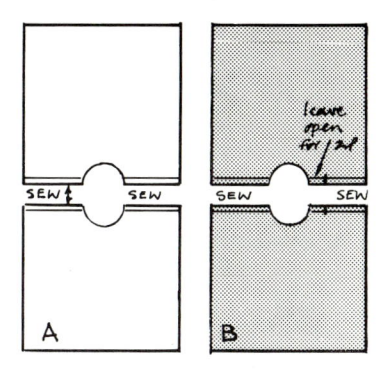

Figure 143

ASSEMBLY SEQUENCE

Figure 144
1. Lay section B on to Section A as shown in Figure 144 and carefully sew waistlines together 0.7 cm in from the edge.
2. Cut through the two layers so that the zip may be inserted – insert zip (see Glossary of basic skills).
3. Cut waistband from the remaining fabric 70 cm × 7 cm.
4. Cut waistband interlining 70 cm × 4 cm.
5. Insert waistband, see Glossary of basic skills and Style 13.
6. Neaten hem. Press.

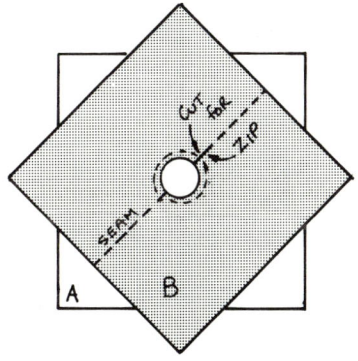

Figure 144

Style 18
Gathered dirndl

STYLE 18

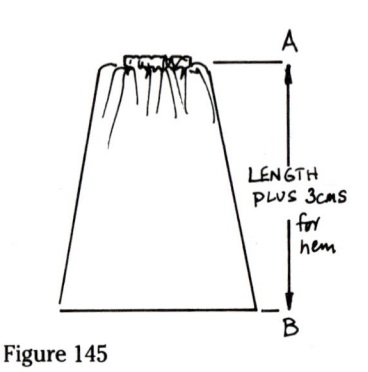

Figure 145

This skirt, which always looks attractive, is extremely simple to sew. It must be made in a soft fabric for it to look its best. The waist should be elasticated and it will fall with soft gathers from the waist.

FABRIC

130 cm of 90 cm wide and 124 cm of lining.

FABRIC LENGTH

A soft cotton for the skirt and a soft lining.

PATTERN

Directly on to the fabric. Measurements given include seam allowances.

TRIMMINGS

None.

CUTTING OUT

See Figures 146 and 147.

MAKING UP

See Figures 148 to 152 and Glossary of basic skills.

MEASUREMENTS REQUIRED

A–B equals skirt length plus 3 cm for the hem allowance. In this example the skirt length is 61 cm plus 3 cm, which equals 64 cm.

Figure 146

The skirt fabric:
Cut two widths of fabric, i.e. 90 cm × 64 cm (will vary according to skirt length).

Note If using a very fine fabric cut three widths for a fuller skirt.

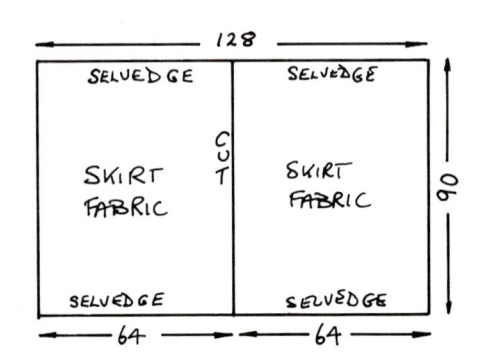

Figure 146

Figure 147

The lining:
Cut the lining in the same way as the skirt, only 3 cm shorter.

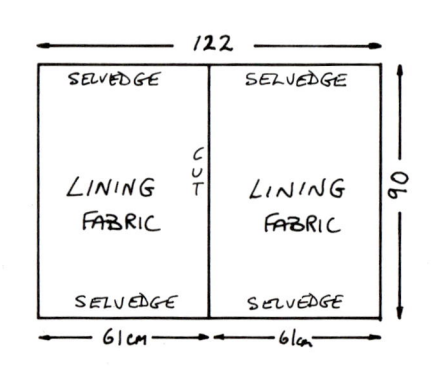

Figure 147

Figure 148

Sew the two skirt lengths together along the selvedge and press the seam open.

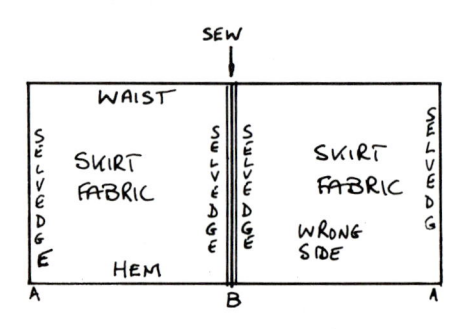

Figure 148

Figure 149

Repeat the process with the two widths of lining. Press open seam.

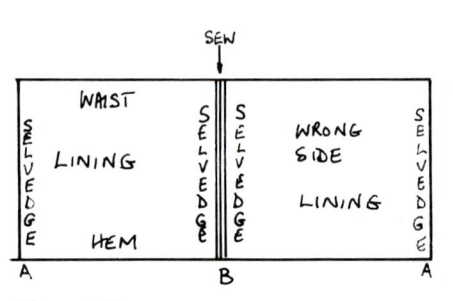

Figure 149

Figure 150

Join the lining to the skirt at the waist seam by sewing a 1 cm seam – press the seam open.

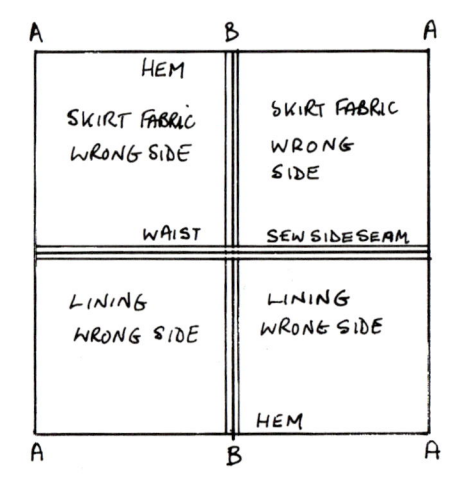

Figure 150

Figure 151

1. Fold the fabric in half as shown in Figure 151 and sew together to form a tube.
2. Turn up a 3 cm hem on the skirt fabric and sew.
3. Turn up a 3 cm hem on the lining.

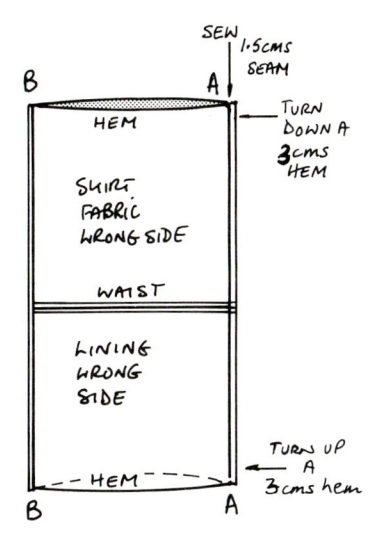

Figure 151

Figure 152

Using elasticated thread on the sewing machine, sew three rows of 1 cm stitches all around waist. See Glossary of basic skills, page 76. Alternatively, thread elastic through a channel for greater strength.

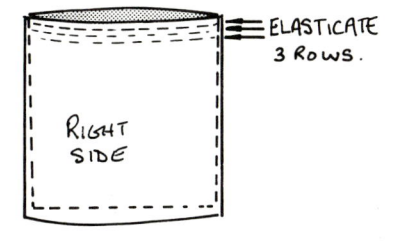

Figure 152

Figure 153

This shows the finished skirt. Press.

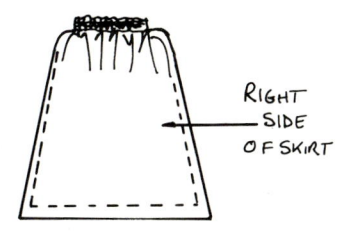

Figure 153

■ ★ ★

Style 19
Harem trousers

STYLE 19

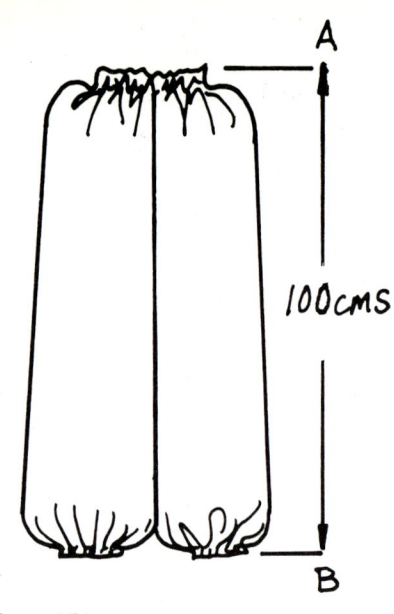

Figure 154

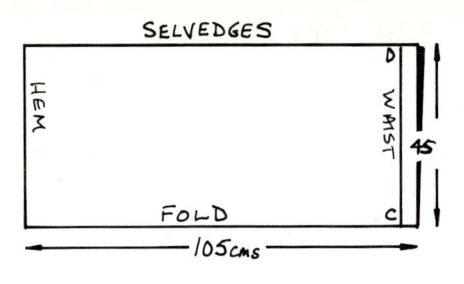

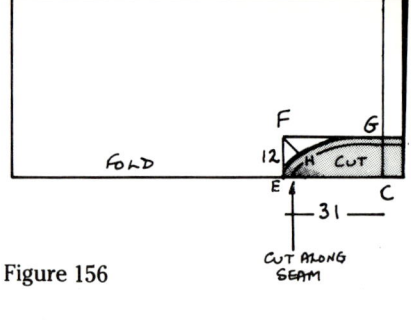

These gathered trousers are for the young and slim.

Figure 155

Figure 156

Figure 157

FABRIC

Chiffon or very fine cotton.

FABRIC LENGTH

2.10 m × 90 cm.

PATTERN

Directly on to the fabric. Measurements given include seam allowances.

TRIMMINGS

Elasticated cotton.

CUTTING OUT

See Figures 155 and 156.

MAKING UP

See Figures 158 and 159.

MEASUREMENTS REQUIRED

1. A–B = trouser length.
2. Body rise – 31 cm in our example. If very tall increase this length.
3. Through measurement.

Figure 155

1. Cut two lengths of fabric 90 cm × 105 cm.
2. Fold one layer of the fabric as shown in Figure 155.
3. Using chalk mark line C–D 2 cm in from the cut edge.

Figure 156

Body rise:
1. Mark point E which is 31 cm down from C at waistline.
2. *Through measurement* E to F = 12 cm all sizes. Connect E to F.
3. Square up to G on the waistline.
4. F to H equals 3 cm all sizes.
5. Connect E to G with a curved line. This will be the trouser centre front and back.
6. Add a 1.5 cm turning to line E–H–G and then cut away the shaded area.
7. Lay the cut trouser on to another layer of fabric and cut out.

Figure 157

This shows the two trouser legs opened out.

Figure 158

Fold the two trouser legs as shown. Sew down side seams with a 1.5 cm turning.

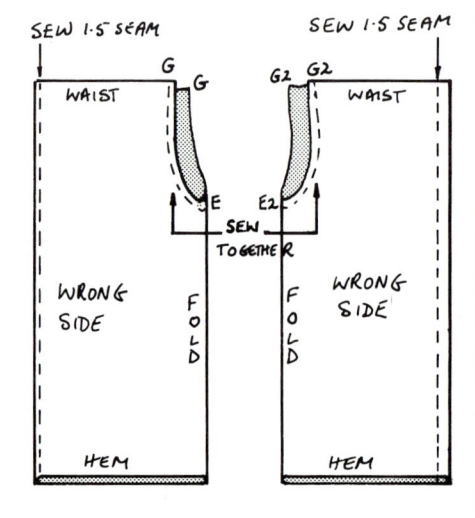

Figure 158

Figure 159
Join G–E–G to G2–E2–G2 for the crutch seam.
Neaten waistline and hem and either insert elastic in the channel or use three rows of elastication to draw up waist and hem tightly to the body. Press.

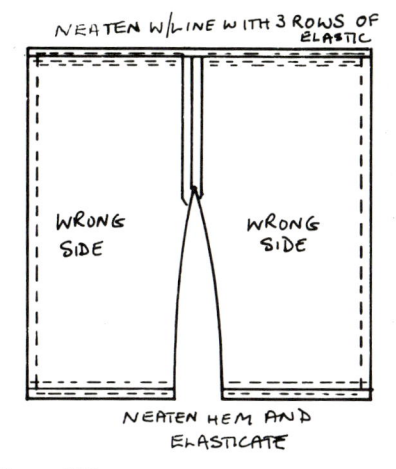

Figure 159

■●★★★

Style 20
Cowl neck blouse

STYLE 20

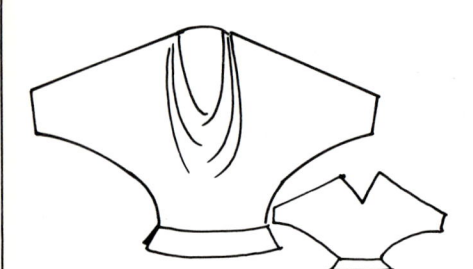

Figure 160

This cowl necked blouse is based on a square with a circle used for the waist. The blouse when draped on to the figure produces a rather daring low necked cowl.

FABRIC

This blouse will only work in a soft jersey.

FABRIC LENGTH

1 m for sizes 10 and 12 of a wide jersey fabric.

PATTERN

A pattern is required.

TRIMMINGS

Hooks and eyes for side opening.

CUTTING OUT

See layout in Figure 167.

MAKING UP

See assembly sequence and Glossary of basic skills.

MEASUREMENTS REQUIRED

Figure 161
1. Waist measurement plus tolerance of 4 cm e.g. 66 cm plus 4 cm = 70 cm.
2. Underarm sleeve length, e.g. 40 cm (not full length).

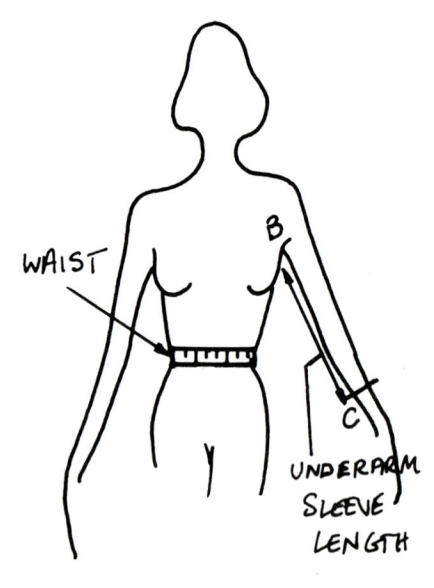

Figure 161

Figure 162
Cut a square sheet of paper 1 m × 1 m.

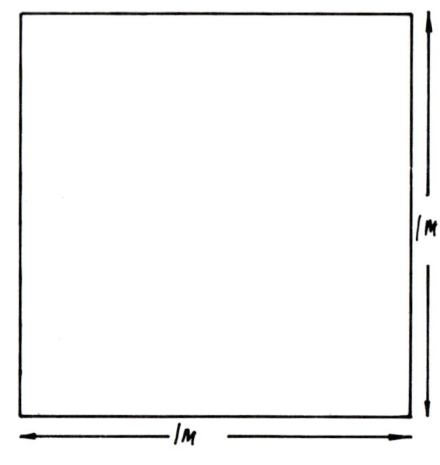

Figure 162

Figure 163
Fold in half diagonally.

Figure 164
Fold again as shown in Figure 164.

Figure 165
To obtain the waist curve use the simple equation shown in the previous styles. For example, the waist measurement
= 70 cm − 2.5 cm = 67.5 cm.
67.5 cm ÷ 6 cm = 11.3 cm.
2. Using the tape measure technique shown in previous styles swing an arc from A with a radius of 11.3 cm.
3. B to C equals 40 cm underarm sleeve length.
4. Square from D to C.
5. D to E = 40 cm (the same as underarm length).
6. Connect E to F (located on line A–F).
7. Cut away shaded areas.

Figure 166
1. Open out the paper pattern and cut away the large shaded area.
2. Cut the remaining half pattern into two halves, one will be the front and one the back.

Figure 167
1. Lay the two pattern halves on to another sheet of paper.
2. *The front*   Simply add seam allowances all around the pattern.
The back   The back has to be reduced so the garment will stay on the shoulders.
3. Fold out a 15 cm dart in the pattern piece as shown in Figure 167. Pin securely. Add seam allowances.
4. Cut both sections out.
5. Mark a notch 12 cm down from the waist. This is for the opening in the underarm to allow the blouse to be pulled over the head.

Figure 168
Cut a rectangle to finish off the waist line 70 cm × 10 cm.

FABRIC LAYOUT

Figure 169
Pin fabric selvedges together. Lay patterns on to the fabric, either mark around the patterns or pin them on to the fabric and accurately cut out.

STYLE 20

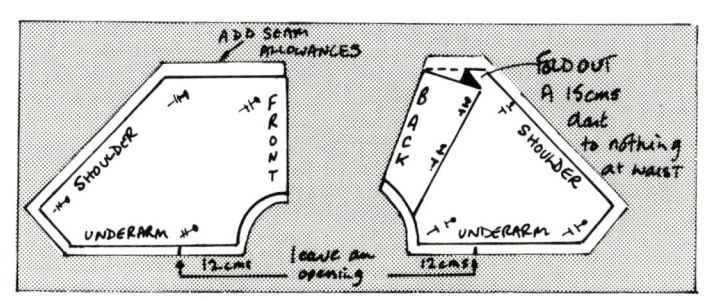

Figure 163

Figure 164

Figure 165

Figure 166

Figure 167

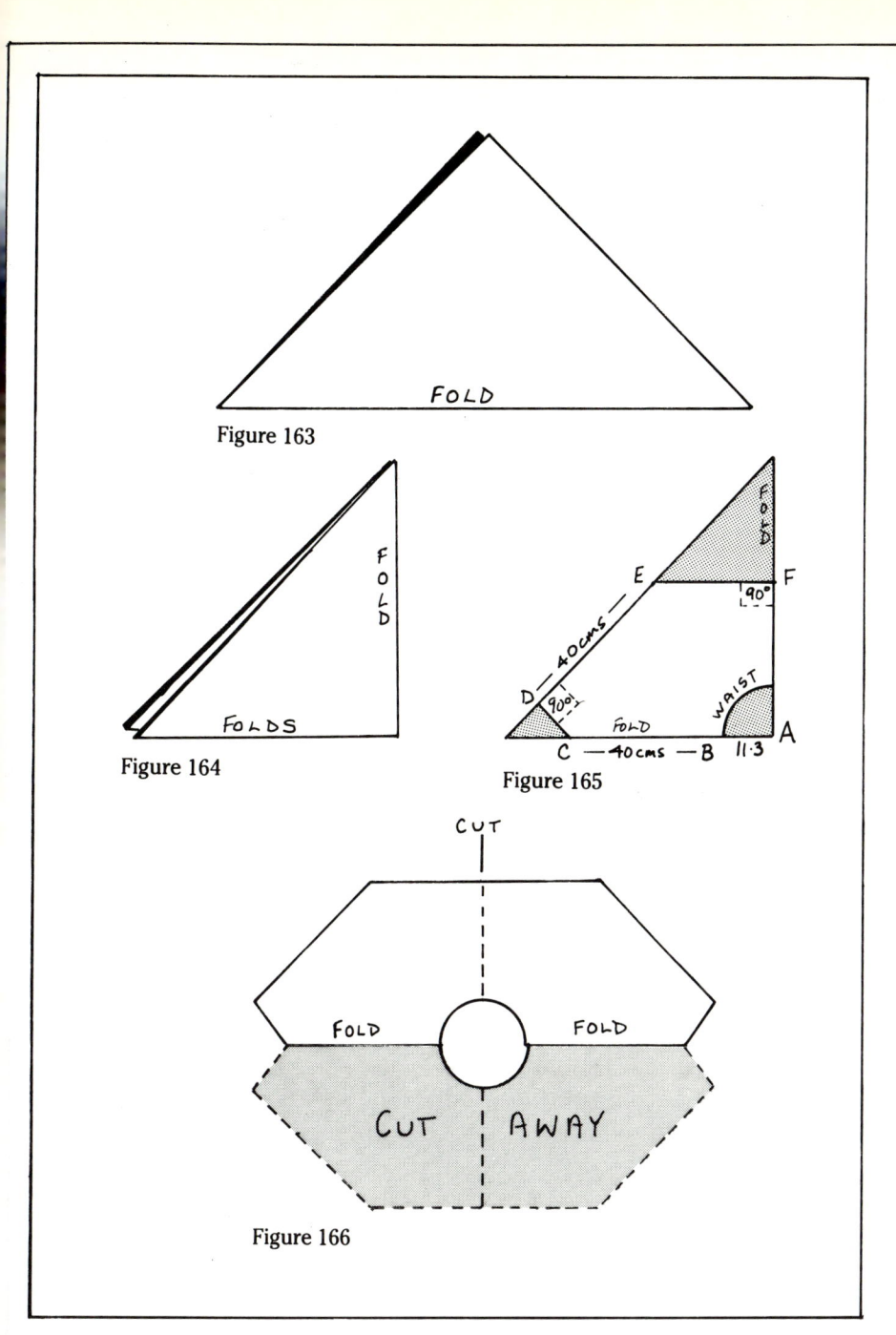

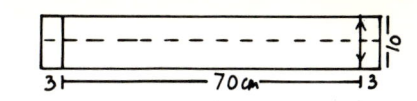

Figure 168

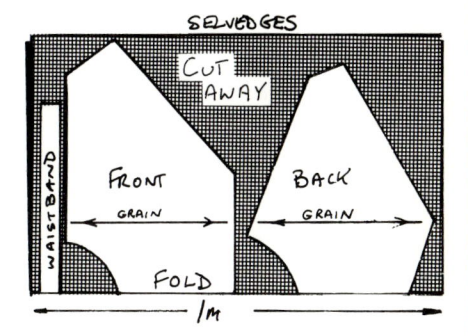

Figure 169

65

STYLE 20

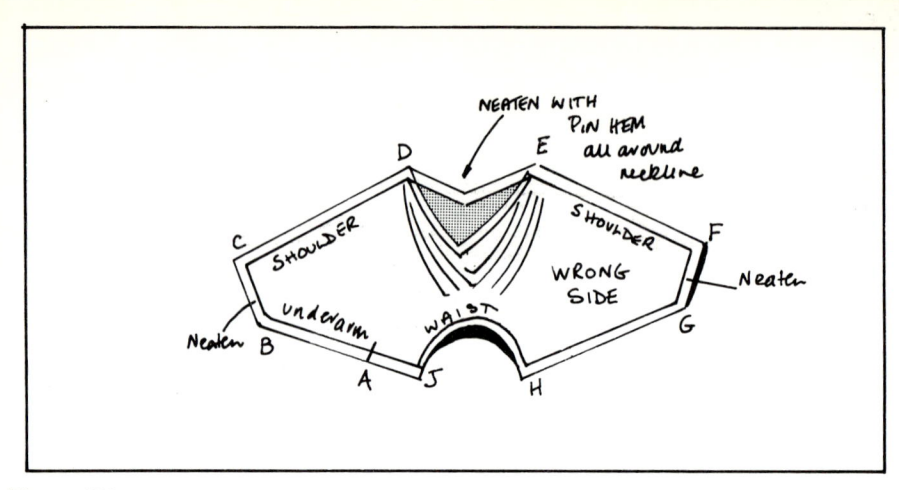

Figure 170

ASSEMBLY SEQUENCE

Figures 170 and 171
1. Lay back blouse on to table.
2. Lay front blouse on top of it, matching shoulder seams and underarm seams. Pin together.
3. Sew from A to B for the underarm seam.
4. Sew from C to D for the shoulder seam.
5. Sew from E to F for the shoulder seam.
6. Sew from G to H for the underarm seam.
7. Neaten the neckline with a tiny pin hem taking care not to stretch the neckline.
8. Neaten both wrists with a tiny hem.
9. Bag out the waistband.
10. Sew waistband to the waist from J to H. See Figure 171.
11. Neaten all seams.
12. Sew hooks and eyes or a fine zip for the left hand opening. Press.

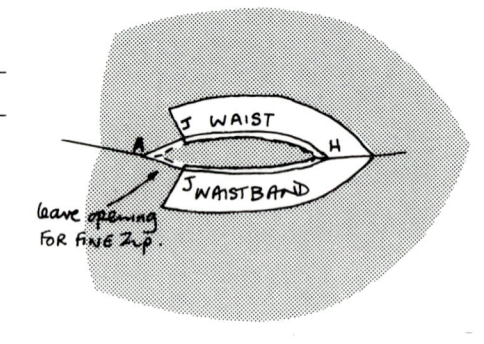

Figure 171

Metric measurements

All the measurements stated in this book are metric measurements. For those who are not familiar with the metric system the following information should be very helpful. It is extracted, with permission, from *Sew Simple*, by Tootal Sewing Products, published by Hutchinson.

METRIC UNITS

A millimetre (written 'mm') is the smallest metric measurement of length. Use it for lengths of less than an inch.
A centimetre (written 'cm') is used a lot in dressmaking. 2.5 cm is about 1 inch.
A metre (written 'm') is the basic metric length measurement. Use it for lengths of fabric.
10 mm = 1 cm, 100 cm (or 1000 mm) = 1 m. Use 2.5 cm for 1 inch. 30 cm for 1 foot. 1 m for 1 yd 3 in (39 ins).

FABRICS

Widths

36 in is equivalent to 90 cm (or 900 mm)
42 in is equivalent to 107 cm (or 1.07 m)
45 in is equivalent to 115 cm (or 1.15 m)
48 in is equivalent to 122 cm (or 1.22 m)
54 in is equivalent to 140 cm (or 1.40 m)
56 in is equivalent to 142 cm (or 1.42 m)
60 in is equivalent to 150 cm (or 1.50 m)
68 in is equivalent to 172 cm (or 1.72 m)
72 in is equivalent to 182 cm (or 1.82 m)

Lengths

Lengths of fabric will normally be cut in the shop to the nearest 10 cm (about 4 in). The usual conversion of fractions of a yard are shown here, and it may be necessary to decide whether to round the required fabric length up or down to the nearest 10 cm.

⅛ yd is about 10 cm
¼ yd is about 20 cm
⅜ yd is about 30 cm
½ yd is about 40 cm
⅝ yd is about 50 cm
¾ yd is about 60 cm
⅞ yd is about 80 cm
1 yd is about 90 cm

Remember that most shops will have conversion charts available and if you are still in doubt ask for advice.

Quantities needed

Some idea of the amount of fabric to buy can be seen below:

Using 140 cm wide fabric:
A coat will need about 2.80 m.
A sleeveless dress will need about 1.4 m.
A dress with sleeves will need about 1 m.
A suit will need about 2.10 m.

TRIMMINGS

Not all items have yet been marked with metric measurements.

Zip lengths

4 in	10 cm	16 in	40 cm
5 in	12 cm	18 in	45 cm
6 in	15 cm	20 in	50 cm
7 in	18 cm	22 in	55 cm
8 in	20 cm	24 in	60 cm
9 in	23 cm	26 in	66 cm
10 in	25 cm	28 in	70 cm
12 in	30 cm	30 in	76 cm
14 in	35 cm		

Sewing machine needle sizes

British	Continental
7	60
9	70
11	75
12	80
14	90
16	100
18	110
19	120

CLOTHING SIZES

Women's wear

The usual sizes (10, 12, 14, 16, 18) are still used but the bust, waist and hip measurements will be shown in metric measurement. Measure the figure with a metric tape measure and round up or down to the nearest centimetre.

Size		10	12	14	16	18
Bust	cm	81	86	91	97	102
	in	32	34	36	38	40
Waist	cm	56	61	66	71	76
	in	22	24	26	28	30
Hips	cm	86	91	97	102	107
	in	34	36	38	40	42

Men's wear

Chest and waist
cm 76 81 86 91 97 102 107 112
in   30 32 34 36 38   40   42   44

Inside leg
cm 74 76 79 81 84
in   29 30 31 32 33

Collars
cm 33 34/35 36 37 38 39/40 41 42 43
in   13 13½   14 14½ 15 15½   16 16½ 17

Children's wear

From 2–12 years, based on height and approximate age.

Height
cm   91   97 102 108 114 121
in   36   38   40   42½ 45   47½
cm 127 133 140 146 152
in   50   52½ 55   57½ 60

Chest
  Approximate age
   2   3   4   5   6   7   8   9 10 11 12
cm 53 55 56 58 61 63 66 69 72 76 79
in 21 21½ 22 23 24 25 26 27 28½ 30 31

67

Fibres and fabrics

FABRICS SUITABLE FOR BEGINNERS

Fabric	Widths cm	Uses	Advantages	Disadvantages	Laundering notes
Calico cotton	90	Overalls, household goods, aprons.	Stays in place and does not slip when sewing. Hardwearing, does not fray.	Cannot be used for fine sewing.	Easy to wash in hot water. Can be starched.
Cambric cotton	90	Handkerchiefs, underwear, blouses.	Soft to handle, will not fray. Is slightly glossy. Suitable for gathering, and presses fairly easily.		White cottons should be boiled.
Cotton, mercerized	90	Dresses, shirts, nightwear, children's wear, blouses.	Presses easily. Can be gathered and tucked. Useful for embroidery. Will not fray. Easy to handle. Usually reversible.		Iron either side whilst damp.
Gingham, cotton or polyester	90	Overalls, housecoats, beachwear, children's garments.	Readily pressed, easy to handle. Gathers well: variety of smocking can be used. Patterned on both sides.	Will not pleat well.	Wash in hot water. Can be starched for extra stiffness. Press whilst damp on either side.
Lawn, cotton or polyester	90	Blouses, dresses, underwear.	Will not fray, crisp but easy to work with. Presses easily, suitable for gathering.		Can be pulled into shape whilst wet. Can be starched.
Piqué cotton	90	Skirts, shorts, jackets, dresses, blouses, collars, cuffs.	Will not fray, maintains shapes and wears well.	Too springy for gathering: ribs should be matched.	Starch to keep crispness. Iron on wrong side whilst damp.
Poplin cotton	90	Children's wear, shirts, bodices.	Will not fray. Firm to handle. Can be gathered and pressed easily.		Iron either side whilst still damp, with hot iron.
Seersucker, cotton or polyester	90	Dresses, underwear, nightwear, blouses, children's garments.	Will not fray. Easy to handle. Very little pressing needed except for seams; will gather; hangs well.	Cannot be tucked or pleated. If pattern is large, care must be taken in matching the seams.	Press lightly if needed, when dry.
Viyella, Clydella and Dayella	90	Blouses, dresses, nightwear, children's wear.	Will not fray. Easy to handle.		Wash in warm water. Iron when dry.

FIBRES AND FABRICS

FABRICS SUITABLE FOR SEMI-SKILLED NEEDLEWORKERS

Fabric	Widths cm	Uses	Advantages	Disadvantages	Laundering notes
Afgalaine	140	Jumper suits, dresses.	Suitable for all types of clothes. Pleats, tucks and gathers well.	Can fray.	Shrinks if washed. Dry clean only.
Bouclé, wool	140 150	Suits, coats, dresses.	Will not crease; lightweight; will drape. Hangs well.	Stitching difficult to keep straight if weave is heavy. Will not pleat easily.	Should be well brushed. Dry clean only.
Chintz	122	Dresses, soft furnishings, housecoats.	Will not fray. Presses easily; hangs well in unpressed pleats.	Cannot be gathered if the glaze is too high. Tough to handle.	Starch when the glaze becomes impaired. Iron on right side when damp. Washes easily.
Cotton, satin	90	Skirts, blouses, dresses, shirts.	Strong, will not fray. Hangs well. Often crease resisting. Presses well. Will tuck and gather easily.		Use hot water when washing. Iron when damp on right side. Glazed surface helps repel dirt.
Crêpe, wool or acrylic	90	Nightwear, dresses, blouses.	Tucks, gathers, drapes, hangs well. Can be embroidered successfully.	Springy.	Press either dry or slightly damp on wrong side with warm iron so that glaze is avoided. Some may only be dry cleaned.
Crêpe de Chine	90	Nightwear, blouses, lingerie.	Easy to handle, will not fray badly. Usually reversible.	Ironed-in creases very difficult to remove.	Irons and washes easily. Iron when damp.
Denim, cotton	90 122	Boiler suits, jeans, shirts, overalls, dresses, dungarees.	Is hardwearing, will pleat well, will not fray; very strong.	Does not gather easily.	May be boiled, iron whilst damp. Normally colour fast.
Flannel, wool	122 140	Suits, dresses, blouses, skirts.	Hangs well; will pleat. Does not fray; suitable for tailored styles.		Wash in warm soapy water. Rinse well. Press on wrong side.
Gabardine wool	140	Suits, jackets, coats, skirts.	For all tailored styles will pleat well; strong material.		Should be well brushed. Dry clean only.
Linen	90 115	Suits, skirts, dresses.	Pleats and hangs well. Presses readily; suitable for tailored clothes. Keeps shape well.	Creases and frays badly.	Washes and presses well. Iron on wrong side unless surface is glazed.
Marocain	90	Evening wear. Blouses for older women. Dresses.	Drapes, tucks, gathers hang well.	Shiny back, so material slips when cut and sewn.	Wash in warm soapy water. Dry clean. Press on wrong side.
Muslin cotton	90	Blouses.	Ideal for fine sewing; can be tucked and frilled.	Will fray.	Will shrink when washed.
Organdie, cotton	90 122	Children's dresses, blouses.	Ideal for fine sewing; can be tucked and rolled. Good for hand or machine embroidery.	Springy, will not gather easily. Frays a little. Transparent.	Irons and washes easily. Iron when damp; can be starched to keep crispness, will shrink.
Sateen, rayon	90 76	Underskirts, linings, for fine dresses of nylon, net or lace.	Other materials can be set over without it clinging	Will fray. Can slip whilst being cut out or during sewing.	Loses much of its body when washed. Can be stiffened with gum arabic.

FIBRES AND FABRICS

Fabric	Widths cm	Uses	Advantages	Disadvantages	Laundering notes
Satin (lingerie) polyester, rayon	90	Lingerie, nightwear, blouses.	Can be gathered, embroidered and tucked. Hangs and drapes well.	Frays easily.	Most lingerie satins can be washed with warm soapy water. Iron on right side when damp.
Serge, wool	140 150	Coats, jackets, suits, skirts.	Will hold pleats. Will not crease easily.		Brush well. Dry clean.
Silk	90 122	Suits, dresses, children's clothes, lingerie, blouses, evening clothes.	Pleats and gathers easily. Very strong but soft material. Ideal for fine sewing, keeps shape. Hangs and drapes well.	Frays badly.	Presses easily. Wild Silk should be ironed when bone dry.
Tweed wool polyester	140 150	Skirts, suits, coats, jackets, dresses.	Will hold pleats. Will not crease easily.	Will fray, can be bulky to wear.	Brush well. Dry clean.
Voile, cotton	90 106	Dresses, blouses.	Good for fine sewing, can be tucked or frilled.	Will fray, make sure seams are strong and reinforced.	Irons, washes easily, needs to be stiffened. Iron whilst still damp.
Wincyette, cotton	90	Nightwear.	Will not fray, strong material, will press easily.		Will shrink, wash in warm water, can be ironed dry or wet.
Worsted, wool	140 150	Skirts, coats, dresses, jackets, suits.	Pleats well, strong material, suitable for all tailored styles.	Clumsy to work on, tends to be bulky. Highly inflammable unless treated.	Should be well-brushed. Dry clean.

FIBRES AND FABRICS

FABRICS SUITABLE FOR SKILLED NEEDLEWORKERS

Fabric	Widths cm	Uses	Advantages	Disadvantages	Laundering notes
Chiffon	90	Blouses, evening wear, neckwear, nightdresses.	Drapes, gathers, and hangs well.	Easily frays. Delicate material which needs skilled handling.	Warm soapy wash. Press with a warm iron.
Georgette, silk, nylon	90	Dresses, blouses, neckwear, lingerie.	Gathers and drapes well. Will not fray easily.	Seams and edges tend to stretch.	Wash in warm soapy water. Press with a warm iron.
Jersey, silk, cotton, wool	102 122 140 150	Blouses, suits, dresses, skirts, coats, trousers.	Drapes and hangs well.	Cut edges tend to stretch. Handle gently so material will not be distorted. Should be sewn with a stretch stitch.	Some need to be dry cleaned. Press along grain so shape will be maintained.
Moiré, taffeta, rayon	90	Evening dresses.	Gathers and flares hang well. Maintains crispness.	Frays badly, water marks. Pattern should be matched at seams.	Dry clean only.
Nylon	90 122	Dresses, children's clothes, lingerie.	Does not need much pressing. Fine but strong.	Frays easily. Transparent.	Washes easily, use warm soapy water. Dries quickly. Do *not* use hot iron.
Taffeta	90	Blouses, petticoats, dresses		Frays badly.	Dry clean. Press wrong side. Glazed on right side.
Velvet, silk, rayon, nylon, cotton		Jackets, dresses, evening wear.	Hangs and drapes well.	Can only be cut in one direction. Not easy to press. Pins tend to mark the pile, so pin with fine needles.	Some need dry cleaning. Corduroy velvet washes well. Press with iron on the wrong side.

Fabrics and Fibres table extracted, with permission, from *Sew Simple*, by Tootal Sewing Products.

Glossary of basic skills

GLOSSARY OF BASIC SKILLS

BIAS CUTTING

Binding is used to finish off the raw edges of necklines and armholes and may be used instead of facings. Binding when cut from a woven fabric is always cut on the bias or true cross of the fabric.

Figure 172
The bias runs at 45° to the warp and weft. Strips of fabric cut at this angle provide the most stretch and are ideal for bias binding which will mould to a curve of a neck or armhole.

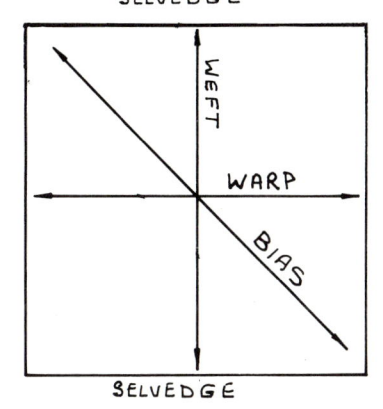

Figure 172

Figure 173
Mark and cut bias strips to the required width, as follows:
(a) Single should be twice the finished width plus two turnings.
(b) Double should be four times to six times the finished width plus two turnings.

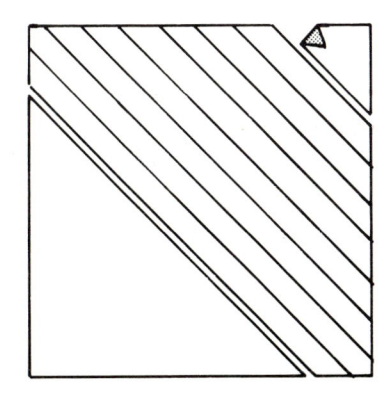

Figure 173

Figure 174
Always join bias strips on the straight grain, i.e. parallel to the warp or weft.

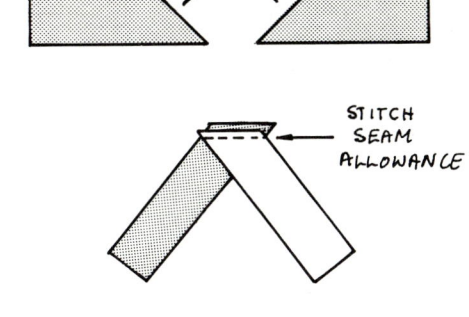

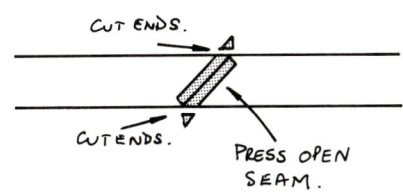

Figure 174

BINDING NECK EDGES

Figures 175 and 176
1. Fold bias in half lengthways, wrong side together. Press in crease.
2. Place bias edges against neck edge (as shown in Figure 172) and *stitch through*. Turn on to right side and stitch.

Note If using joined strips, place joins at shoulder seams or centre back if possible.

Figure 175

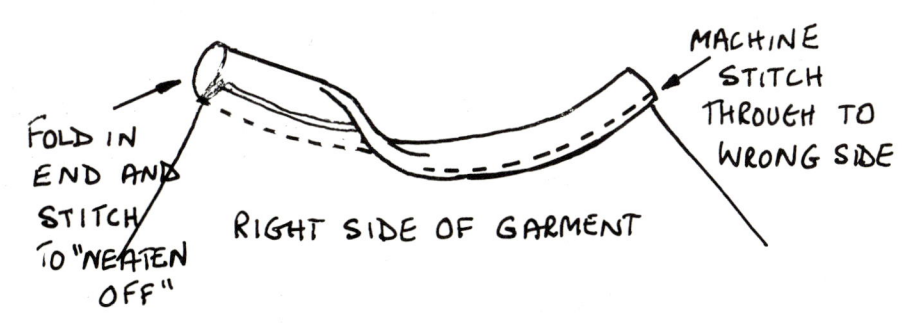

Figure 176

BOUND EDGE FINISH

Figure 177
Finish off seams that may show by encasing each raw edge with either crossway or purchased double-fold bias binding.

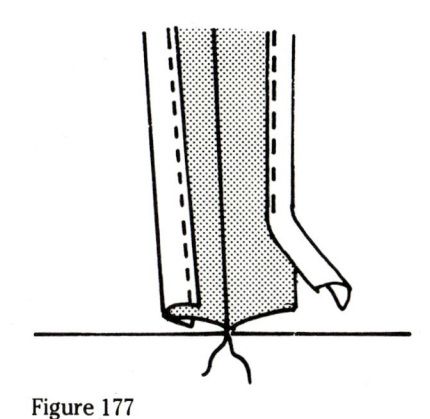

Figure 177

FABRIC LAYOUT

Each style in this book has a diagram which shows how the pattern should be laid on to the fabric in order to use as little fabric as possible. However the following general rules should be helpful.

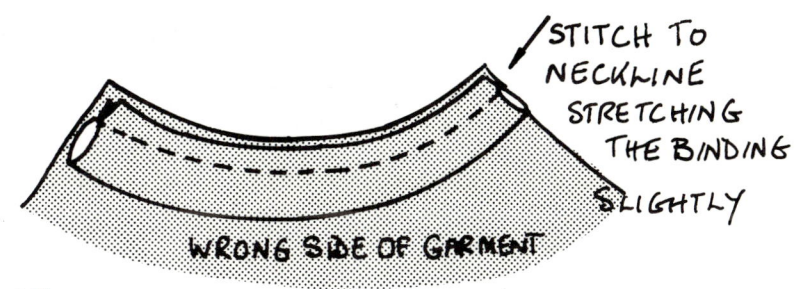

GLOSSARY OF BASIC SKILLS

1. Check that all the pattern sections are marked up with grain lines and notches.
2. Check that all pattern pieces are present and correct.
3. Fold the fabric accurately and make sure that it is not 'off grain'.
4. Place each pattern section on to the fabric as indicated in layout diagram.
5. Pin each pattern section on to the fabric accurately, largest pieces first. (If a fine fabric is to be used, pin within a seam allowance so that pin marks will not show.)
6. Check that all pieces are on the correct grain before cutting out.
7. If the fabric has a pile (for example, velvet) or is a one way check or plaid, it is essential to lay the pattern pieces all facing the same way. The pile should brush downwards from the neck to the hem. This may mean that the garment will need more fabric than a two way fabric. In this case ignore the layout diagram and replan according to the fabric width.

Figure 178

8. (a) Stripes must match around the body.
(b) Prominent stripes should be positioned on the garment for the best effects.
9. Cut out carefully with very sharp shears.

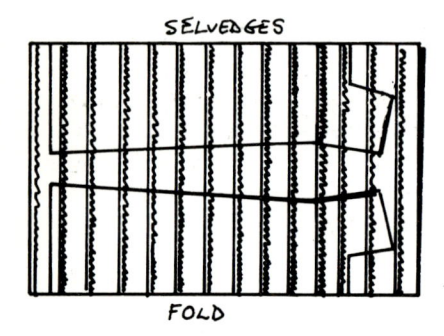

Figure 178

FACINGS

Facings are used to neaten raw edges, to reinforce and to stop cut edges stretching.

PATTERN CUTTING A NECK FACING

Figure 179
1. (a) Fold a sheet of paper.
(b) Lay the pattern on to it.
(c) Draw around the neck.

Figure 179

Figure 180
2. Remove pattern and draw in lines 5 cm at neck and front.
3. Cut out facing and open out pattern.

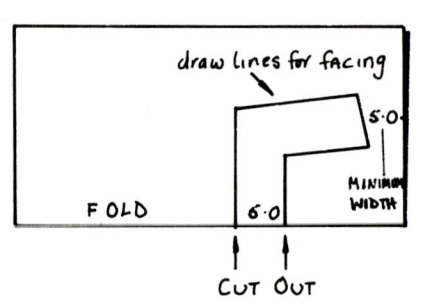

Figure 180

Figure 181
4. Repeat process for the back neck facing. Use these patterns for the interlining if used.

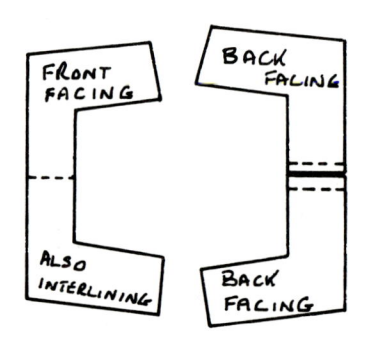

Figure 181

SEWING

1. Iron interlining on to wrong side of facings.

Figure 182
2. Place back and front shoulders of facings together (right sides) and sew a 1 cm seam.

Figure 182

Figure 183
3. Press seams open and neaten edges.

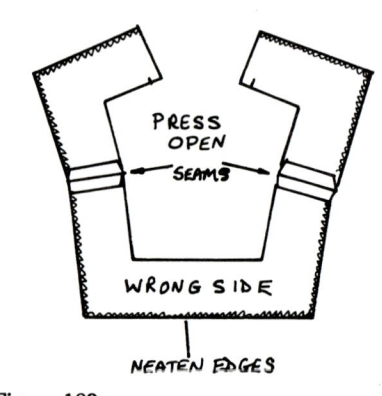

Figure 183

Figure 184
4. (a) Pin right side of facing to the right side of the garment accurately.
(b) Machine around neckline through both thicknesses.
(c) Snip corners.
(d) Turn facing through to the inside of the garment.
(e) Press.

Note See zip section for attaching to the facing at the centre back.

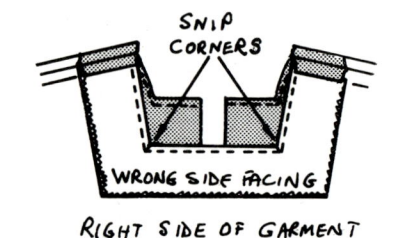

Figure 184

GLOSSARY OF BASIC SKILLS

GATHERING (MACHINE)

Figure 185
1. Set machine to longest stitch and loosen top tension.
2. Machine two or more rows of evenly spaced stitching.
3. Draw up bobbin thread.
4. Ease bobbin thread through fabric and evenly distribute fullness from both ends.
5. Each end of drawn-up thread should be wound, a pin placed at right angles to the stitching.
6. When gathers are even, fasten off with thread ends, by making several back stitches to secure gathers.

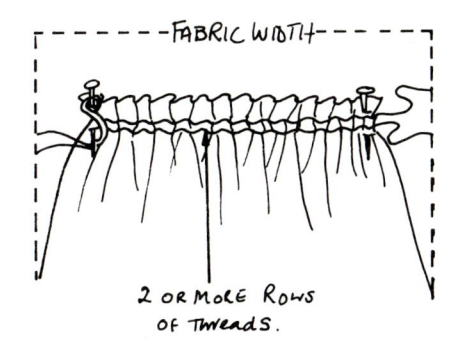

Figure 185

GRAIN

A successful garment must be cut on the appropriate grain so that it will hang correctly and will not twist or drop and the fabric pattern will appear evenly positioned on the garment.

Figure 186
1. This figure shows the grains on a woven fabric. As a rule each pattern section has a grain line marked on to it. The grain line is always laid on to the warp, i.e. parallel to the selvedge.

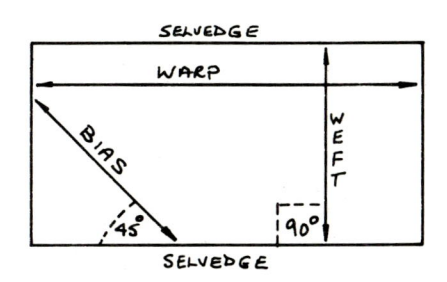

Figure 186

Figure 187
2. The warp, wherever possible, runs down the centre front and centre back of the garment. This adds strength to the garment and helps to prevent the hem from dropping. Each pattern section must have a grain line drawn on to it.
Sections A and C are cut on the straight grain.
Section B is cut on the cross.

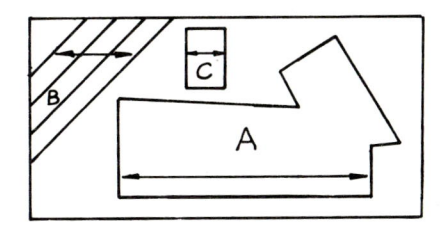

Figure 187

HEM FINISHES

NARROW MACHINE HEM

Figure 188
Suitable for circular skirts and sleeves and for fabrics that do not fray.

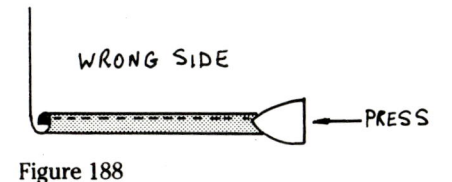

Figure 188

IRON ON SEAM BINDING

Figure 189
Suitable for all types of garments.

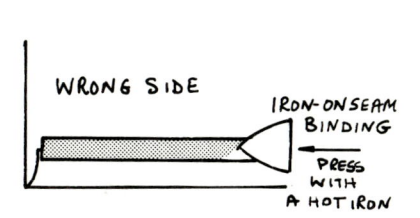

Figure 189

SLIP HEMMING

Figure 190
Suitable for skirts with reasonably deep hem.

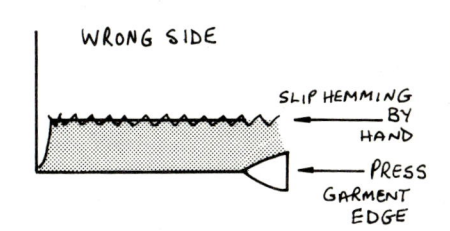

Figure 190

INTERLINING

Interlining or interfacing is used to add body to specific garment areas such as necklines, openings, cuffs, belts, collars etc. and is sandwiched between facing and the garment. Interlinings come in various weights ranging from the very soft to the tailoring weights which are usually much heavier. Interlining can also be woven or non-woven and also fusible or non-fusible. The choice for each specific garment will depend on the fabric and the garment section to be interlined. The instructions in each style indicate the pattern piece which should be used to cut the interlining.

SEAM ALLOWANCES

The following seam allowances are recommended as average for the fabric used. However, alter them according to your own preferences and type of seam finish used.

	Cotton type	Knitted
Shoulder	2.0	1.5
Armhole	1.5	1.5
Waist	1.5	1.5
Styled seam	1.5	1.5
Side seam	2.0	1.5
Hem*	1.5–5.0	1.5–5.0
Waistband	1.0	1.0
Cuff	1.0	1.0

* The narrowest hem for the widest shape

GLOSSARY OF BASIC SKILLS

Seam allowances must be added accurately to the finished sewing line so that accurate pattern cutting will be transferred to the finished garment. Each exercise indicates exactly where and how much to add to each seam. There are many methods of neatening seams. The following are the most common and can be used for the styles in this book.

PINKING

Used for fabrics that do not fray.

Figure 191
1. Sew up seam.
2. Press seam open and then use pinking shears to neaten edges.

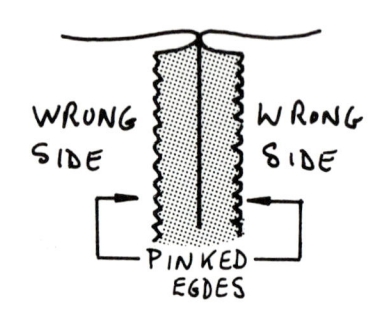

Figure 191

MACHINE NEATENING

Used for fine to mediumweight fabrics.

Figure 192
1. Sew seam.
2. Roll 0.5 cm inwards and sew through all thicknesses.
3. Press.

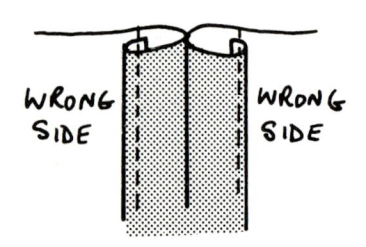

Figure 192

OVERLOCKING

Used for all types of fabrics.

Figure 193
1. Sew seam.
2. Use a sewing machine to neaten edge.
3. Press open.

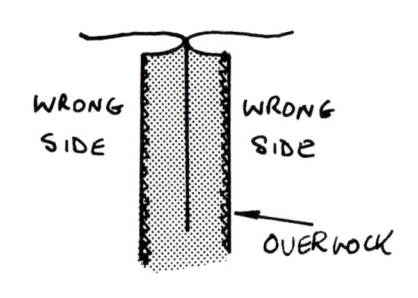

Figure 193

BOUND SEAM

Use for fabrics that have a tendency to fray.

Figure 194
1. Sew seam.
2. Sew a binding around seam – as shown in Figure 194.

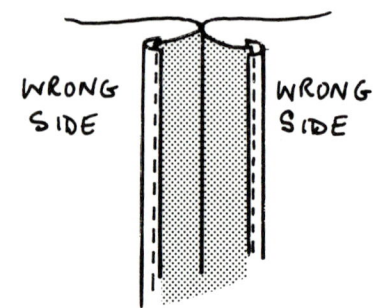

Figure 194

SHIRRING

Figure 195
1. Shirring elastic should be wound on to the machine bobbin.
2. Use a long stitch.
3. Mark the place where the rows should be.
4. Machine from the right side, holding the fabric taut.

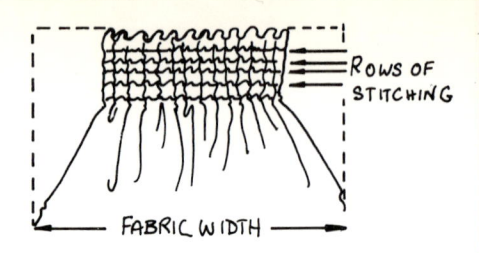

Figure 195

SLIT OPENING

Figure 196
1. Cut facing, see page 74. Interline front and back neck facings and join at the shoulder seams. Press open. Sew facing around the neck. Mark centre front slit and sew around it as shown in Figure 196.

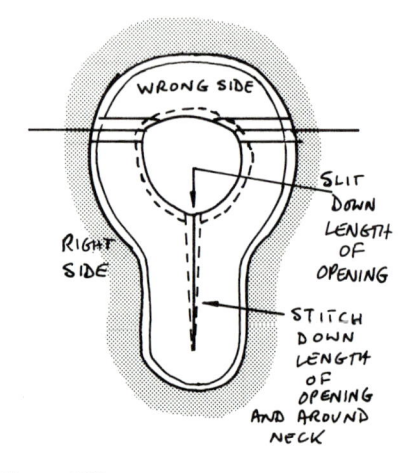

Figure 196

Figure 197
2. Turn facing inside the garment, press and top stitch.

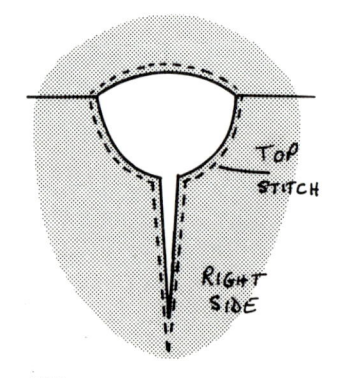

Figure 197

GLOSSARY OF BASIC SKILLS

TIE BELT

Figure 198
1. Cut the tie to the measurements listed in the style. Join the fabric if required. Cut interlining and fuse with an iron to the wrong side.

Figure 198

Figure 199
2. Fold belt in half (lengthwise) and press. Stitch as shown in Figure 198 leaving 3 cm open.

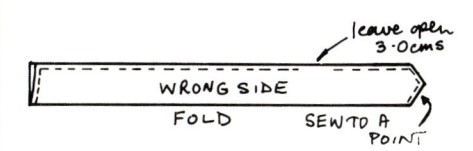

Figure 199

Figure 200
3. Turn through to right side via the unstitched area left open and stitch all around. Press.

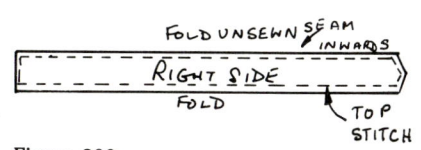

Figure 200

WAIST FINISHES FOR SKIRTS

There are many ways of finishing the raw edges at the waist. The following two methods are suitable for the styles in this book.

WAISTBAND

Figure 201
1. Follow the instructions contained in each style for the measurements needed for the waistband. Cut the interlining and press to the wrong side of the fabric.

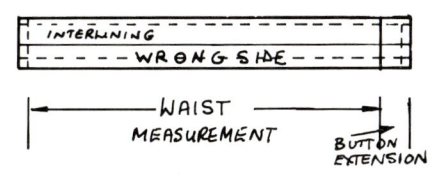

Figure 201

Figure 202
2. Fold waistband as shown in Figure 201 and stitch ends.

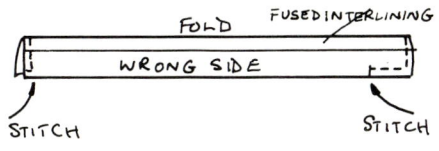

Figure 202

Figure 203
3. Turn waistband through to the right side.

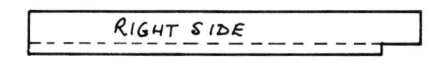

Figure 203

Figure 204
4. Stitch the right side of the band to the wrong side of the garment.

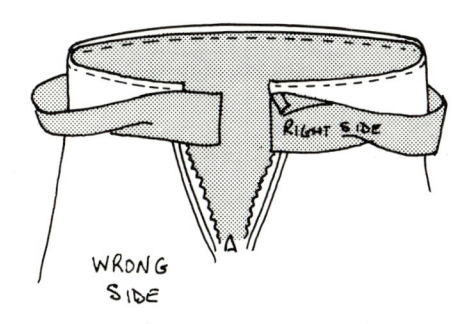

Figure 204

Figure 205
5. Pull waistband upwards and working from the right side of the garment turn under the seam allowance and topstitch.

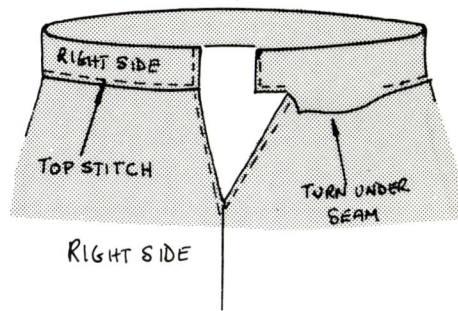

Figure 205

PETERSHAM

Petersham can be used to face the waist edge. It provides a firm, clean finish.

Figure 206
1. Shaped petersham must be used. Apply to the waist and sew as shown in Figure 205.

Figure 206

Figure 207
2. Fold the ribbon to the wrong side of the garment and sew on hooks and eyes.

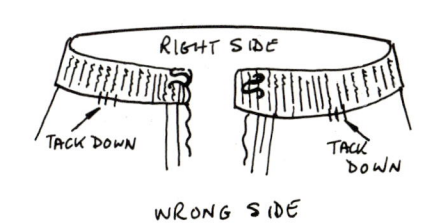

Figure 207

77

GLOSSARY OF BASIC SKILLS

WRIST FINISHES

SEPARATE FACING

Figure 208
1. Sew facing into a ring. Press seam open. Sew on to sleeve with right sides together.

Figure 209
2. Turn on to the inside of the sleeve and edge stitch. Press.

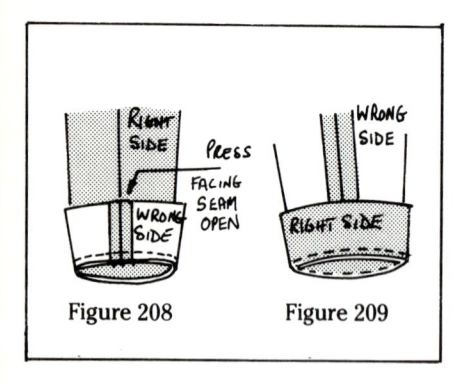

Figure 208   Figure 209

GROWN-ON FACING

Figure 210
1. Add 4 cm to 5 cm to sleeve end. Fold sleeve and sew seam. Press seam open.

Figure 210

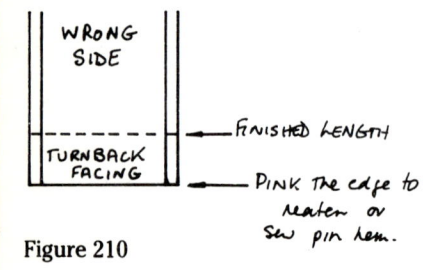

Figures 211 and 212
2. Turn facing inwards and catch to the seam by a tack. Press.

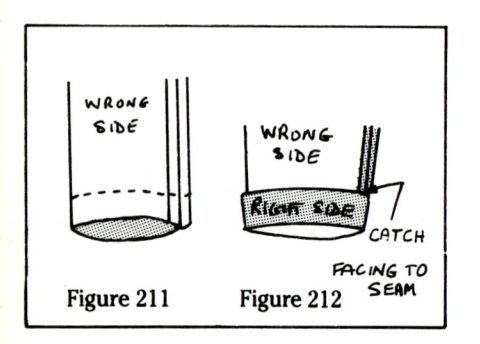

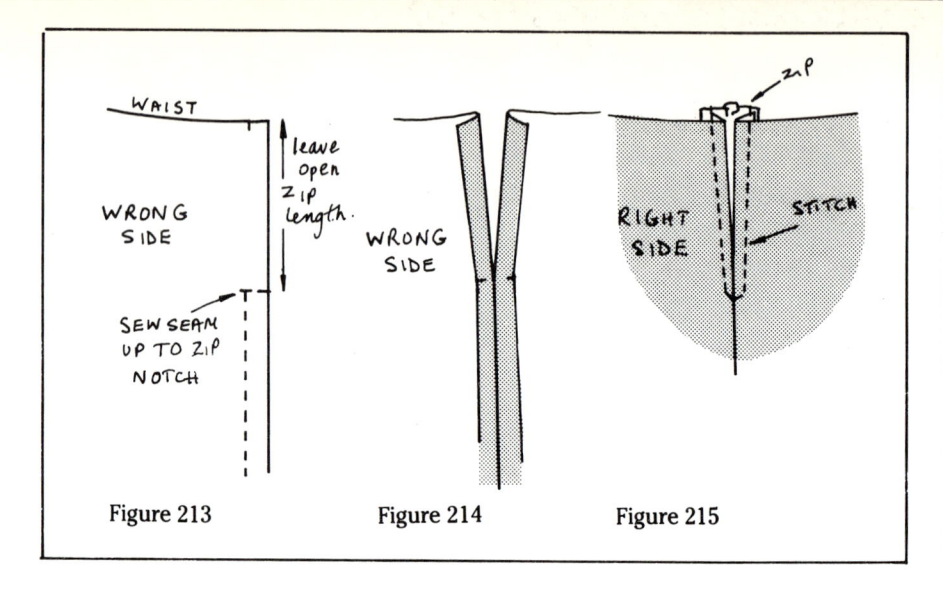

Figure 211   Figure 212

Figure 213   Figure 214   Figure 215

ZIP SETTING (SIMPLE)

Figure 213
1. Sew seam up to zip notch, which should leave open the length of the zip.

Figure 214
2. Press seam open.

Figures 215 and 216
Lay on to zip and sew through evenly.

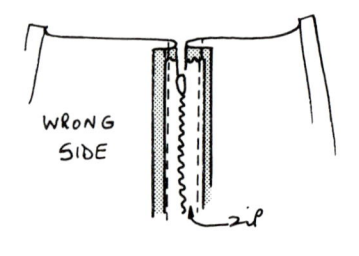

Figure 216

ZIP GUARD

Zip guards are used in garments to protect the zip from being damaged, by preventing underwear and linings from catching in the zip.
Cut the guard the length of the zip plus seam allowances by the width of the extension.

Figure 217
1. Pin zip guard to the open seam on the wrong side of the garment.

Figure 218
2. Sew through. Press.

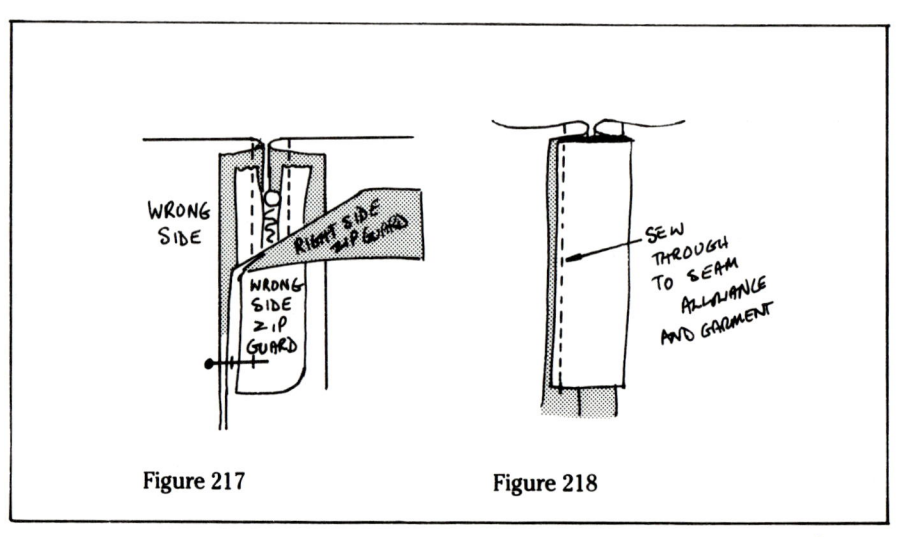

Figure 217   Figure 218

Specialist suppliers

Morplan, Garment Trade Supplies Service
56 Great Titchfield Street
London W1P 8DX

Franks
Market Place
London W1P 8DY

Further reading

Sew Simple: A step by step guide to dressmaking, Tootal Sewing Products (Hutchinson)
Pattern Cutting and Making Up, The Professional Approach, Volumes 1–3, M. M. Shoben and J. Ward (Batsford)
Decorative Dress and Fashion, Gwyneth Watts (Hutchinson)